Stanley Fish,
America's Enfant Terrible

The Authorized
Biography

Stanley Fish,
America's
Enfant Terrible

Gary A. Olson

Southern Illinois University Press ■ *Carbondale*

Southern Illinois University
www.siupress.com

Printed in the United States of America

19 18 17 16   4 3 2 1

Jacket illustration used with permission from Stanley Fish

Library of Congress Cataloging-in-Publication Data
Names: Olson, Gary A., 1954–
Title: Stanley Fish, America's enfant terrible : the authorized
    biography / Gary A. Olson.
Description: Carbondale : Southern Illinois University Press,
    2016.
Identifiers: LCCN 2015028119| ISBN 9780809334766
    (hardback) | ISBN 9780809334773 (e-book)
Subjects: LCSH: Fish, Stanley Eugene. | Critics—United
    States—Biography. | Educators—United States—Biography.
    | Lawyers—United States—Biography. | Scholars—United
    States—Biography. | Intellectuals—United States—Biography.
    | United States—Intellectual life—20th century. | United
    States—Intellectual life—21st century. | BISAC: BIOGRAPHY
    & AUTOBIOGRAPHY / Educators. | BIOGRAPHY & AUTOBIOGRAPHY /
    Literary.
Classification: LCC PN75.F57 O47 2016 | DDC 801/.95092—
    dc23 LC record available at http://lccn.loc.gov/2015028119

Printed on recycled paper. ♻

*For Lynn Worsham, a true intellectual, and my
best friend, companion, and soul mate*

Contents

Preface

This is a chronicle of the life and work of Stanley Fish. A legal scholar, literary critic, and public intellectual, Fish is considered one of the twentieth century's most original and influential literary theorists. He has taught at Berkeley, Hopkins, Columbia, Duke, the Cardozo School of Law, and many other institutions, and currently he is the Davidson-Kahn Distinguished University Professor of Humanities and a professor of law at Florida International University. Until recently, he was also a weekly columnist for the *New York Times*.

In *Justifying Belief: Stanley Fish and the Work of Rhetoric*, I tell the story of my first introduction to Fish, or at least to his reputation. The story is worth retelling here. I was a graduate student in a Milton seminar, and our professor was an unusually animated and entertaining performer who would race around the room reading passages from *Paradise Lost* in a dramatic tone and who insisted that we imagine the epic as the prototype of modern superhero comic books. We were to envision Satan as a caped archenemy, springing from here to there with fiendish energy. Needless to say, our professor did much to make Milton come alive, even for the most jaded among us. At the opening of class one day, he burst into the seminar room brandishing a copy of Fish's *Surprised by Sin*. The book had begun to cause a furor not only among Miltonists but among many in English studies, and our instructor had just finished reading it. Even though we were accustomed to his frenetic teaching style, nothing could have prepared us for the vociferous agitation he unleashed on us that day. Slamming the book down on the seminar table, his bald head glowing red, he sputtered uncontrollably as he spit out his words: "This book is an abomination! This is *not* how you read Milton, and it's *not* how you do literary criticism! Don't waste your time and money on such drivel!" (As might be expected, we all immediately and surreptitiously ordered our own copies of this forbidden fruit to discover what magic resided there.) Throughout the remainder of the semester, our instructor would signify an errant reading of a passage from Milton by snarling, "That sounds Fishy to me!" Ever since that day, Fish's works have become required reading for me, as they have for countless others.

As it turned out, this Miltonist's vehement reaction to Fish's book was characteristic, if somewhat overplayed, of how many readers received this groundbreaking work of criticism. And the controversy did not end there; from that time onward, Fish's work has always polarized readers, and he quickly developed a reputation as the academy's bad boy—a true enfant terrible.

Because Fish has a following well beyond the confines of literary studies and enjoys a wide lay audience of educated readers, I have attempted to create here a hybrid: a combination of a literary biography and a more traditional account of a life. I imagine a mixed audience: one that is composed of academics interested in the progress of his career as a scholar, but also nonacademics who have read one or more of his books or *New York Times* columns and who are curious about who he is and what he has done. This, then, is more a reportorial narrative than a scholarly treatise, so I have purposely avoided citing specific works or passages from them, and I employ no footnotes or scholarly apparatus. This is a story. A true story, but a story nonetheless.

My intent was to write neither a tribute to nor a condemnation of Fish. Although I have not always agreed with key points and positions Fish has taken, especially the line of reasoning set forth in *Professional Correctness* and extended in *Save the World on Your Own Time*, it is not my intention to make an assessment of his work nor to be judgmental about him or his life. My stance is that of the observer. I am simply reporting what I have learned, and I hope the story I tell sheds some light on him and his life.

The primary source of information for this work is hundreds of hours of recorded interviews (and some correspondence) with friends, enemies, colleagues, former students, family members, and Fish himself. A number of individuals interviewed for this work requested that they not be identified, and I have respected their wishes and have not named them here. I also spent many hours in the Stanley Fish archive—an extensive collection of his papers, letters, and other materials—housed at the University of California at Irvine Special Collections and Archives.

Many people generously corresponded and spent time with me discussing their memories of various times in Stanley's life. I would like to thank all of them and in particular the following: Kenneth Abraham, Paul Alpers, Bette Bottoms, Rachel Brownstein, Seymour Chatman, Steve Cohn, Chris Comer, Bill Covino, Mitchel Craner, Reed Dasenbrock, Peter Fish, Ronald Fish, Michael Fried, Donald Friedman, Jerry Graff, Stephen Greenblatt, Stanley Hauerwas, Betsy Hoffman, Fred Jameson, Brit Kirwan, Richard Lanham, David Lodge, Walter Michaels, Hillis Miller, Ron Paulson, Alan Pearlman, John Presley, Barbara Smith, George Starr, Michael Tanner, Astrida Tantillo, Jane Tompkins, and Ken Wissoker. They are in no way responsible for any infelicities or factual errors that may have crept into this book.

I would also like to thank the dedicated personnel of the East Providence Historical Society, the Rhode Island Historical Society, the Rhode Island Jewish Historical Association, and the University of California at Irvine Special Collections and Archives. I would also like to thank Mike Morgan and Joyce Strobel of Daemen College for their expert artistic and technical assistance. Work on this project was supported in part by the Idaho Humanities Council and by the Office of Sponsored Research and the College of Arts and Letters at Idaho State University.

Finally, I would like to thank Stanley himself for graciously making himself available for countless hours of sometimes uncomfortable questions and for making available to me family photos for this book.

Gary A. Olson
Amherst, New York

Stanley Fish,
America's Enfant Terrible

Chapter 1

Beginnings:
The Fish Family and Friends

T he year was 1991. Hundreds of spectators—university students, professors, community members—crowded into the large auditorium and anxiously awaited the evening's event. Every seat had already been taken, and it was still fifteen minutes until showtime. Disregarding the prominently displayed signs from the fire marshal, spectators began to sit on the floor of the two main aisles, stretching from the first row to the very back of the auditorium. Others stood in the back until not a single person could squeeze into the room. Latecomers stationed themselves just outside the room at the two theater-style doorways, hoping that they would be able to hear the speakers when the event began.

This was the first in a much-publicized series of public debates on multiculturalism between conservative author Dinesh D'Souza and academic superstar Stanley Fish. The event was billed as the academic world's equivalent of a heavyweight title match in boxing. It was the height of the culture wars, and the air in the auditorium at the University of South Florida in Tampa crackled with excitement and anticipation.

In an office suite down the hall from the auditorium, the university president was holding court. He stood before the two debaters, a hand on one shoulder of each, while deans and other dignitaries encircled the trio. "I'll be introducing you two fellows tonight. Now, don't hold back any punches," he instructed the combatants. "The crowd expects a knock-out blow. Get out there and give'm everything you've got."

An entourage of university officials escorted the trio down the hallway and through the auditorium's stage entrance. As the speakers strode out into the spotlight, the crowd erupted into a paroxysm of applause and cheers. It was as if the crowd had gathered not to hear some academic debate but a rock concert or a talk by a film star.

This scenario was familiar to Stanley Fish. He had reached the pinnacle of a distinguished career, and he frequently filled auditoriums when he spoke. Some considered him the most famous American academic of the century. Others thought of him as the nation's most prominent "public intellectual," a description he himself rejected. One thing is certain: he has consistently remained one of the nation's most controversial intellectuals.

His work has always polarized readers. While one critic credits him with being "one of the very best essayists in any field" and with exhibiting "dazzling intelligence," another declares that he is "crass" and that his work is "intellectually sullying" and "morally disgusting." His work seems to elicit either admiration or disdain—rarely anything in between. There simply is no such thing as a tepid response to Fish's work. Fish is intentionally provocative in his works—hence the strong feelings he elicits from readers. An enfant terrible, he persistently challenges sacredly held positions, arguing, for example, that as one of his titles puts it, "There Is No Such Thing as Free Speech—and It's a Good Thing, Too," or that we may believe that we operate by high principles but we really do not because there will always be a point where we will compromise a principle for some other goal, or that we may feel that we fully support multiculturalism or cultural tolerance but this too has limits because there will always be a cultural practice—genital mutilation, say, or honor killings—that we simply cannot abide. These and other positions articulated by anyone else might simply be dismissed, but the fact that one of our most celebrated intellectuals argues them carefully and even brilliantly is what causes such cognitive dissonance for so many readers.

In many ways, the life of Stanley Eugene Fish has been a Horatio Alger story: a working-class boy from Providence, Rhode Island, makes it big through sheer will and hard work. Symbolically, it is fitting that he grew up in Providence. The city (and surrounding territory) was settled in 1636 by Protestant theologian Roger Williams, who had been banished by his fellow Puritans from Salem, Massachusetts, after he spoke out repeatedly against some of the political and religious views of his colleagues, decrying rampant superstition and intolerance. Williams and his followers fled to what now is Rhode Island and purchased from the Narragansett Indians a substantial tract of land at the head of Narragansett Bay and the Providence River, promptly naming this future settlement "Providence," presumably because Williams felt that his God was directing his fate. Like Williams, Fish has always been quick to criticize superstitions or any beliefs that seemed to be misguided. (He once summed up his work this way: "From my point of view, there are a lot of people out there making mistakes, and I'm just going to tell them that they're making mistakes.") Both were men of strong and unwavering convictions, and neither suffered fools lightly. While not an outcast like Williams, Fish has always been a renegade in his own right. Very much the loner, he is someone who has always set his own agenda, kept his own counsel, and is generally not seen as one of a group (the deconstructionists, for example, or the antifoundationalists). Ironically, Williams (b. 1603) was a contemporary of John Milton (b. 1608), the English poet and essayist whose work Fish made his life's passion. Like Williams, Milton was a staunch Protestant, and both were outspoken critics of injustice.

During the first quarter of the twentieth century, the city that Roger Williams had founded over two and a half centuries earlier was now a thriving hub of commerce. Merchants and industrialists enjoyed a flourishing and rapidly expanding economy. The city had gained a reputation for producing a diverse range of high-quality goods, from heavy machinery to fine jewelry. These years were perhaps Providence's most prosperous. Enough wealth was produced to benefit many—but not all—of its citizens, from the opulent industrialists to the ethnically diverse working-class laborers who toiled in the countless foundries and retail establishments that seemed to spring up overnight throughout the region.

This diverse mix of hardworking immigrants helped Providence gain its reputation as an exemplar of good old-fashioned New England work ethic. Like a number of other cities in New England, Providence became home to populations of immigrants who tended to settle in separate sections of town. The Italians—and there were many of them—formed their own enclave, principally in what is still known as Federal Hill. The Jews, Portuguese, Eastern Europeans, and other groups (including a sizable Arab population) all formed their own communities and contributed to the growth and prosperity of the city. Providence in those days lived up to its name: it was truly a boomtown, as if watched over by some beneficent deity. One of its nicknames in those days was "The Divine City."

During that quarter century, the Providence skyline took on a distinctively metropolitan aspect as modern high-rises and skyscrapers began to jut into the New England sky, topped off by the majestic Industrial Trust Building (which was completed in 1928), symbolizing that the modest city of Providence, the capital city of the nation's tiniest state, had finally come of age. It seemed to many at the time that there could be no end to this economic exuberance. The sky's the limit.

These were the years and the context in which Stanley's parents, Max Fish and Ida Weinberg, would meet, court, and later marry and raise a family. Max was born in Poland in 1909. His father emigrated to the United States in the early 1920s and labored long hours painting houses and taking on odd jobs in order to save enough money to send for his wife and two sons, which he did in 1923. Ida Weinberg was born in 1914 in Rhode Island. Her parents had emigrated from Russia to England and then to the United States. She was the daughter of a furrier, a lucrative occupation in the 1920s. Max, in contrast, was an unschooled plumber's apprentice under the tutelage of his uncle, Frank. When Max began courting Ida, some in her family felt that he was not an appropriate suitor for Ida, that she would be marrying beneath her educational level and social class were she to accept the plumber's proposal. The young couple eventually won the family over, and they were married on April 7, 1932. The newlyweds took up residence on Somerset Street in a working-class section of South Providence. They encountered many hardships but were happy together.

The prosperity, growth, and exuberance of Providence during the 1920s were not to last beyond the decade. The Great Depression—which had begun in 1929, three years before Max and Ida had married—was especially cruel to Providence. Manufacturing, which accounted for its initial prosperity, began to decline. Foundries closed, downsized radically, or moved south to take advantage of nonunion labor. The ranks of unemployed swelled as a result, leading to the closure of countless other businesses because so many unemployed citizens had no money to purchase the goods that would have kept those businesses afloat. The city and county governments suffered from the resulting precipitous loss of tax revenue. Many citizens left the state, further reducing the government's tax income. The once prosperous and up-and-coming city was struggling for its very existence. The city experienced unprecedented poverty and decay.

Providence was still reeling from the effects of the ongoing Depression nine years later when Stanley Eugene Fish was born, on April 19, 1938. He was Ida and Max's firstborn child and a cause of great celebration throughout the extended family. Max was twenty-nine, Ida twenty-four. They were very much in love. The new infant boy brought much joy to Ida and Max and seemed to make all the hardships of their life worth enduring.

Max would leave the employ of his uncle, a disagreeable man by all reports, to labor as a steamfitter in the naval shipyards. This job enabled Max and a coworker to save enough to strike out on their own. They would traipse through the working-class neighborhoods, fixing toilets, unclogging sinks, plunging drains, and taking on any plumbing jobs their fellow immigrants had for them. Eventually Max would establish his own business, naming it the Max Fish Plumbing and Heating Co. He worked hard, and the business flowered. Soon he had a reputation as an honest and competent professional, and people throughout the city were eager to patronize his business.

The devastation of the Depression was extensive, but this was only the first of a one-two punch that would send Providence to the floor. Five months after young Stanley was born, on September 21, what became known as the Great New England Hurricane of 1938 roared through Providence, sweeping cottages and modest houses from their foundations, flooding much of the city with a giant storm surge, and devastating the already struggling town. The once-promising town was ruined—at least for the foreseeable future. The hurricane was the coup de grâce, wiping away many of the businesses that had managed to survive the Depression and wreaking a level of physical devastation that would take many years, even decades, to recover from. This was the milieu in which the infant Fish began his life.

The first eight years of Stanley's life were spent in a rough working-class neighborhood in South Providence. Bars punctuated the city blocks, and the local bullies would occasionally accost him on his mile-and-a-half-long walk from his home on Bogman Street to and from elementary school, sometimes with painful consequences. The long, lonely walk day in and day out was a fraught time for Stanley; he could never know in advance whom he would encounter at the next turn, what vicious bully, what group of thugs, what older boy looking to solidify his reputation as someone to fear if not respect. Some of this bullying was anti-Semitic, as roughnecks would taunt and attack the young Jewish boy. Stanley never sought out fights because he knew that he did not possess the kind of strength or skill to be attempting to beat people up. In what would later become a well-honed character trait, he would try to talk himself out of these difficult encounters, and on more than one occasion he was successful.

Other than the daily challenge of safely navigating the city streets, these early years were uneventful for Stanley. He fondly remembers studying dinosaurs at school, and he also took violin lessons. The music teachers decided that since he was taking violin lessons, he should have a seat in the school orchestra. This was not a good idea. Despite the lessons, he had no aptitude for playing music, so, in characteristic Stanley Fish style, he faked it, drawing the bow gracefully across the strings but without actually allowing the bow to touch them. It's not clear to this day if anyone ever caught on to his ruse.

Stanley was the eldest of the four Fish children; he had a sister and two brothers. His sister, Rita, was nearly three years his junior, and he was especially close to her. She dated boys of his age, so they frequently appeared at the same social gatherings together. Rita was smart, outgoing, very beautiful, and exceptionally popular. She would go on to become an early-childhood educator, and for a while she served as the head of an exclusive day-care school in New York City where many children of Columbia University professors would attend. At that time she was studying for her PhD in education at Columbia. Sadly, she would not complete her degree because her husband purchased a yacht supply business in Miami and they relocated. She had loved New York City, so the adjustment to life in hot and humid Florida was difficult, but she did eventually adjust and became the head of a Miami preschool for many years. She died of cancer in 2009.

His brother, Ronny, was eight years younger than Stanley. The entrepreneur of the family, he was industrious, imaginative, and hardworking.

As a child, he was a bit of a terror in the neighborhood, causing disruption whenever possible. Frequently, he would instigate encounters with his older brother and would end up getting a good punch for his efforts. Once, Stanley observed that his younger brother was attempting to "get his goat," so rather than wait for the scenario to play out its natural course, Stanley walked over and socked him in the arm. "What did you do that for?" his brother blurted out indignantly. "Well, you were just going to try to get me to hit you anyway," he replied, "so I thought I'd just cut to the quick." Ron would later go into the family business in place of Stanley and would build the business up after Max semiretired. Then, when he was forty-seven and after he had successfully managed the business for nearly two decades, he sold it and moved to the island of St. Kitts in the Caribbean, where he purchased a substantial parcel of land with stunning views of the Caribbean and built a community of thirty villas, selling for a quarter of a million dollars each. He dubbed this community Half Moon Bay Villas. (His brother Peter teased him by calling it Ronny-wood.) After he sold the thirty villas that comprised the community, he purchased an even more gorgeous property on a hill, right at the edge of where the Caribbean and the Atlantic Ocean meet. On this tract, he built a community of luxury villas ranging from three to ten million dollars each, and he called the community the Estates on Sundance Ridge. Of course, he built himself an estate as well, with breathtaking views of the Caribbean out one side and the Atlantic out another and the main part of the island with its little mountain peaks out a third. He spends his days building estates, swimming in the ocean, and taking his fishing boat out for pleasure. He would regularly sell his catch to the restaurants in town—not that he needed the income, just for fun.

His other brother Peter was the artistic genius of the family. Because he was eighteen years Stanley's junior, the two brothers did not grow up together. Stanley had already gone off to college when young Peter was growing up, but they did spend time together at family events, and they quickly developed a genuine admiration for one another. Peter would later become a six-time Emmy Award–winning composer, producer, and jazz keyboard player. For several years he was considered the most performed composer of television soundtracks because he had produced background music for so many programs, from news shows to dramas to scores for HBO movies. He also headed a jazz band that plays in

New York City called the Peter Fish Group and a rock band called CTA (California Transit Authority) that he formed with the original drummer from the band Chicago, Danny Seraphine.

In 1946 the family abandoned the rough streets of South Providence and moved to the top floor of a two-family home on Lancaster Street, a much more respectable neighborhood in the Lower East Side. This new community straddled a tough working-class area on one end and a middle-class neighborhood on the other. As a consequence, this new area was a mixture of both. Many of the families on this block were on their way up socially and economically. The residences were mostly two-story wood houses with a family living on each floor. One of Stanley's close boyhood friends lived next door in the upper flat, and below them lived a young couple that had recently opened an upscale men's clothing store, a novelty at the time in Providence. These young entrepreneurs were in their late twenties at the time, and the wife had the beauty and poise of a movie star; all the boys pined for her.

At the end of the street closest to the more upscale neighborhood stood a neat but unpretentious house not unlike most of the houses on the block. It exhibited no pomp or embellishments, no conspicuous displays of wealth, yet its residents were indeed wealthy. This was the residence of Raymond Patriarca, an influential Mafia leader who later would become the head of the New England Mafia, one of the twelve dons of La Cosa Nostra. By the time the Fish family moved to the neighborhood, Patriarca had already served a prison term for robbery and was considered a ruthless and vicious criminal. Like the rest of the neighborhood in the 1940s, Patriarca was on his way up. In the early 1950s he would become one of the most feared and powerful Mafia dons in the country, exerting control over organized criminal activities throughout all of New England. He lived in this corner house with his wife and his son, Raymond Jr., who later would succeed him as don.

Mrs. Patriarca and Ida were co–den mothers of the local Cub Scout troop at the time, and Mr. Patriarca would constantly invite Max and Ida to go out with his family or to accompany them on vacations. Max and Ida would then scramble to invent credible excuses as to why they could not go. Nevertheless, the two families became quite close, and Stanley's brother Ron palled around with Raymond Jr. In one instance, Ida, who by all accounts was quite a character, happened to be driving by the Patriarca residence with Stanley in the car. She spotted the don-to-be in his driveway, pulled to the curb, rolled down the window, and shouted, "Hey, Raymond. How many bodies have you got buried under that driveway?" The don, who was intently hacking away at a hedge with clippers, simply winked in reply. Anyone else would have paid dearly for such macabre humor, but Ida's strength of personality and the friendship between the two families inoculated her.

Moving to this new neighborhood was a good change for Stanley. He had traded the bullies, anxiety, and hardships of his previous existence for a supportive and largely Jewish community peopled by many children of or near his own age. While Lancaster Street was a relatively short street, extending for only two city blocks, more than twenty kids lived in the homes on one of the two blocks (between Camp Street and Ivy Street), and they formed a tight-knit group of friends. In many ways, Stanley's life really began with this move. He found friendship, camaraderie, and support. The family occupied the second-story flat, and Stanley's Aunt Gertrude (Ida's sister) and Uncle Irving lived below them and became an important part of his support network.

The neighborhood was composed predominantly of conservative Jews and a smattering of reform Jews, although everyone attended the same conservative temple nearby in the neighborhood. The Fish family members were practicing Jews. They went to synagogue once a week and observed the High Holidays; they were all conscious of being Jewish and of being part of a Jewish community. These were the years directly after World War II, so the entire community had a heightened awareness of the Holocaust, of how things could have been even worse for Jews had it not been stopped, and, most important, of how the whole tragedy could happen again. These realizations produced an intense sense of community; everyone felt an obligation to protect one another, as if they were all family—and in so many ways, they were.

Stanley attended Hebrew Sunday school, learned all the usual stories, listened intently to the rabbi. One Sunday school lesson had an indelible effect on him. Rabbi Eli A. Bohnen—who later would officiate at his first wedding and who is credited with being the first Jewish chaplain in the U.S. Army to help liberate the Dachau concentration camp—was addressing the class. He said in his kind but commanding voice, "Do you want to know what being honest means? Here's what being honest means. You're at a pay phone. There's nobody else around. Suddenly the pay phone disgorges some coins. You know the money doesn't belong to you, but nobody's watching. What do you do? You don't pocket the change. An honest person will try to find out whose money this is and return it to him. *That's* what being honest means." Stanley never forgot that lesson. At the age of thirteen, he was bar mitzvahed, and he sang not only his own part of the ceremony, but also some of the cantor's part. He had a good voice then, before it changed. So, religion played an important part in his formation, not so much in making him devoutly religious, but in providing him a moral compass and, perhaps as important, a sense of community and belonging.

Both Ida and Max had extremely powerful personalities, so life in the Fish household was seldom serene. Ida played an active role in encouraging her children to excel and in managing the household in general. She was demanding, high-strung, and had a volatile personality. She had a hot temper and constantly subjected people to bickering, nagging, and sometimes even badgering. On more than one occasion, she became so enraged at one of her neighbors that she stormed over to the person's parked car and ripped the antenna from it.

Each of the four siblings in turn would seek to strike out on his or her own as soon as possible, mainly to escape Ida. One of the boys thought of her—perhaps hyperbolically—as "evil"; another as "insane." When the youngest of the four, Peter, was only eleven years old and had had an especially trying encounter with her, Stanley and his other brother Ron took Peter aside and said emphatically, "As soon as you can leave this home, you *must* get out." Peter took their advice; when he was fifteen he left and moved in with his brother Ron. For better or worse, it was Ida's spirit that permeated the household; this was both a positive, in that she gave life, excitement, and animation to everyone's daily existence, and a negative, in that her manic personality was the source of much stress and anxiety in the household.

In contrast, Max—like so many males of his generation—was emotionally absent for much of the time. He would return from work and read his newspaper or just sit silently in his favorite easy chair. When he was in social situations, however, he became exceptionally lively and a skilled storyteller. Those who knew him thought of Max as an extraordinary character, a very powerful figure with penetrating blue eyes. He was a man of considerable personal presence. Part of this presence was physical—he was a large-framed, muscular man—and part of it was his very commanding personality. People instantly liked and respected him, and he was a powerful role model for Stanley, who adopted many of Max's attitudes and character traits. Despite Max's influence as a role model, father and son were not close. Max did not believe in small talk, and he kept to himself when not in social settings. At home he remained aloof, taciturn, and unapproachable—that is, when he was not arguing with Ida. During the summers of 1953 and 1954, when Stanley was fifteen and sixteen years old, the family leased a small cottage on the seashore, an hour's drive from Providence. Stanley worked for his father during those summers, and the two would commute in to Providence in the morning and back to the cottage in the evening. As long and monotonous as the drive was, Max would not utter a word during the entire trip. For Max, no talk was always better than small talk. It's not that the two had a chilly or strained relationship. After all, Max was grooming Stanley, his eldest son, to take over the family business one day. And despite the lack of communication, Stanley remembered his father with fondness. He had great respect for Max and thought of him as a man of immense integrity. It's just that Max was the epitome of the "strong and silent" male, and he made no effort to engage with his children; that was their mother's job.

Max was never reticent, however, when he felt the need to lay down the law or discipline one of his children. Once when Stanley was quite young, he pushed his baby sister's carriage off the porch—with her in it! Fearing the consequences of his offense, he immediately sought refuge in a locked bathroom. A massive man, Max stood for a moment outside the bathroom, giving his son the opportunity to unlock the door. Hearing no response, Max, with one powerful swing, knocked the door in. This patriarch might have locked his children out of his emotional life, but no one would lock him out of his own bathroom.

Max was extremely kind and generous, especially to relatives. One of Stanley's uncles on his mother's side of the family once worked for Max until Max offered to set him up in his own business. Later, he would refuse to be paid back for his generosity. He also paid to bring several relatives—some of them Holocaust survivors—to the United States from Europe. On multiple occasions he even bailed out from financial difficulties various members of Ida's side of the family—the very individuals who opposed Ida's "marrying down" by her taking up with him in the first place. He never bragged about these good deeds. In fact, he never mentioned them to anyone. His mother was known to comment in private, "My poor Max. They're bleeding him dry."

Despite his flaws, Max was an excellent provider. A hard worker, he made sure that Max Fish Plumbing and Heating Co. was the best of its kind in the region. Early on, he had transformed the business from a simple repair shop to a heating and plumbing contractor business. His big break came in 1948 when he won a bid to remodel the heating system and restrooms of a large synagogue in Providence. There was no turning back from that point; it soon became one of the largest heating and plumbing firms in southern New England, and Max rose to the top of his field, becoming the president of the plumbing contractors' association. By the time Stanley was a sophomore in college, in 1956, Max and Ida were able to purchase a fashionable house on Abbottsford Court in a very desirable section of town: the Upper East Side. It was a beautiful single-family house, on a lovely tree-lined street. Stanley remembers noting his grandfather's intense pleasure in first seeing the new home and his pride that his son had become so successful that he was able to own such a respectable house on the Upper East Side.

Decades later, when Stanley himself was successful and at the top of his own field, Max told a chilling tale of his own youth. It was 1923, and Max, then fifteen years old, and his brother would be leaving Poland for the United States the next morning. They were suddenly attacked in the street by a gang of anti-Semitic thugs and viciously beaten. Later that evening Max slipped out, found a large stick, and hunted down one of his attackers. Max would only say that after he was finished with his attacker, he had no idea if he was still alive. Stanley would recount this story in what became one of his best-loved *New York Times* columns: "Max the Plumber."

With Ida and Max having such forceful personalities, the Fish household often erupted in contentious bickering and arguing. A next-door neighbor commented wryly that if you lived next door to the Fish family, you didn't need a television set; you just opened the window, sat back, and listened. That was better than any TV drama or situation comedy. The fighting and quarreling was not just between the two parents but also between Ida and Stanley. They constantly fought and shouted at one another, and this mode of engagement would last throughout their lives, even as adults. They would fight about almost any and every subject. Max referred to it as a clash of wills between two extremely willful people. Once, when a teenager, Stanley got into an especially explosive argument with his mother. He leapt into the family car and Ida ran toward him, so he locked the doors and started the engine. Willful as ever, she grabbed onto the driver's side door handle—as if to say, "You're not going anywhere, buster." Equally as willful, Stanley threw the car into gear and proceeded down the driveway, dragging her with him. Eventually, she let go, and he drove into town, where he had a clerical job in the layaway department of a department store. An hour later Max strode authoritatively into the layaway department, thrust out his hand, and demanded, "the keys." Stanley sheepishly surrendered the keys, and without saying another word, Max wheeled around and walked away.

Stanley found this incessant clamor distressing, and to cope with it he would find every occasion to withdraw and seek comfort in his neighborhood friends, usually in marathon card-playing sessions. He liked to play poker and gin rummy, and he became quite skilled at both. He was so eager to escape the family bickering that he would even convince his parents to allow him to stay home while the rest of the family would go on vacations. Thanksgivings were especially trying. The family and assorted relatives would gather for a traditional celebration, and inevitably it would erupt into paroxysms of recriminations, name-calling, and hurt feelings. While Stanley hated this family contentiousness and did much to escape it, it was formative and would later have a profound effect on his first marriage and on how he conducted himself as an intellectual.

Perhaps in part to escape his tumultuous home life, Stanley developed a lifelong passion for sports. Intensely competitive, he would play each game as if it were his last, and he continued this same intensity throughout his life. He played every sport—football, baseball, softball, track. When the streets would ice over, he would play hockey. He even tried his hand at golf, but it bored him. Growing up, he would watch televised Major League baseball whenever he had the opportunity. He thought of it as a beautiful and elegant game. Ted Williams was his baseball hero. In those days especially, but even to a certain degree in our own time of satellite-broadcast sports games, most New England baseball fans fixated on the Boston Red Sox. Not to do so—say, to root for the Yankees—was tantamount to treason or, worse, apostasy. Williams was one of the Red Sox's brightest stars, and it is easy to see how he captured the imagination of the young boys of the time. Stanley also attended hockey games of the local American Hockey League team that were played in the arena not far from his neighborhood, and occasionally he would go to the dog track. Basketball, however, was his special passion. He began playing it at age eight and was still playing pickup games in his seventies. As a youth he was short and somewhat thickset, but he did not let this become much of an obstacle to his athletic endeavors.

Once in the early 1990s I helped bring Stanley to my campus to give a university-wide talk. I called him a week before he was to arrive and asked if he minded paying a brief visit to my department and talking informally to the faculty, who would be eager to hear words of wisdom from one of the nation's most prominent scholars. I fully expected him to offer to do it for an honorarium, if at all. Instead, he said, "I'll do it on two conditions: (a) if you arrange for me to play a basketball game with faculty or students, and (b) if you arrange a tennis match for me." He must have been fifty-five years old at the time, but you wouldn't have known that from his performance on the basketball court: with ease he wove in and out of the faculty members—all thirty-somethings—that I had arranged to play the game. The game was hard fought and intense. I sat in awe as he performed maneuvers that would have been impressive coming from someone half his age. While the tennis match was equally hard fought and intense, I have to admit that I played a trick on Stanley. The partner I had chosen for him was one of my colleagues. He was slightly older than Stanley, but he had once played semipro and had maintained his game through the years. He was a dynamo. Stanley didn't have a chance, but he reported that he very much enjoyed the challenge.

Young Stanley enjoyed a large, tight-knit group of neighborhood friends, but he was especially close to a small inner circle. Perhaps his closest friend was his next-door neighbor, Stanley Bleeker; they spent much time together, often in the company of Ralph Posner and two cousins, Stevie and Harry Saltzman. Of keen interest to Stanley was a girl who lived at the end of the street, Betty Eisenberg. She was stunningly beautiful with long dark hair, penetrating eyes, and a slim, well-toned physique. The two dated for a while. A special friend in the group was Bobby Roy, who lived three houses down the street. Bobby was in the same class with Stanley at Classical High School. He was a state golf champion, was captain of the basketball team, was voted the class's best dressed and best looking, and was one of the most popular of all his peers. Stanley and Bob would end up both going to the same college: the University of Pennsylvania, where they continued their close friendship. The preoccupations of this group were sports and card playing—for money, of course. They spent every spare moment indulging in one or the other. When it came to cards, however, no one could match their crony, Alan Pearlman. He seemed to have an innate skill for reading the cards. Playing with him always generated some mixture of admiration and frustration. Stanley was a competent card player, but Alan was in a wholly different league. He was such a pro that, after completing a successful career as a lawyer, he would retire to become a professional gambler, moving to Connecticut so that he could be near the Foxwoods Resort Casino in Mashantucket, which is operated by the Mashantucket Pequot Tribal Nation. This group of young Jewish boys and girls grounded Stanley, gave him his sense of confidence, belonging, and emotional support. He would never forget them.

While Stanley's father was an important role model for him as he grew up, so too was Ida's youngest brother, Paul. He was three-and-a-half years older than Stanley, and he took a special interest in his nephew. A handsome boy, he was a football player in high school, very popular among his peers. In 1950, at the dawn of the Korean War, he joined the Air Force and received training in a revolutionary new technology: computers. All of this—his status as a football hero, his career as a dashing Air Force officer, his expertise in a sexy new technology that few people had in those days—greatly impressed Stanley, and he looked up to his young uncle with admiration. Sadly, Paul would make a strategic mistake: after leaving the Air Force, he chose not to capitalize on his specialized knowledge of computers and instead went into real estate sales. His career was less than successful, and he was plagued by a number of diseases, including emphysema. In a kind of role reversal, Stanley would repay him for his kindness years later. The then jet-setting academic would seek him out whenever he was scheduled to give a talk in the Rhode Island or Massachusetts areas. He would always make sure that his ailing uncle was invited to the event and sometimes would have a car sent for him. After the talk they would go out to dinner with whatever professors were hosting the talk. Stanley was proud that although his uncle had attended only two years at a business college, Bryant College of Business Administration, he nonetheless held his own in conversations with the high-level academics. He was one of Stanley's favorite relatives.

Stanley was not bookish. He was more likely to play basketball or gin rummy than to read, but he did read for pleasure. He liked to visit his mother's sister, Gertrude Chase, and her husband Irving in the downstairs flat and borrow books from their modest library of popular stories. He especially liked tales of Paul Bunyan and the Knights of the Round Table.

Unlike his sister and brothers, who attended the neighborhood public high school, Hope Arts School, Stanley and his cronies all attended Classical High School, a high-quality college-prep school in Providence that to this day prides itself on its rigorous curriculum. Most graduates of Classical go on to obtain college degrees, and the school is often cited as one of the highest-performing high schools in the nation. On more than one occasion Stanley has stated that the education he received at the yellow-brick Classical High School was more rigorous than that of the two Ivy League universities he attended, Penn and Yale. Among its distinguished alumni are several governors of Rhode Island and American author and humorist S. J. Perelman, not to mention Stanley. Some would think that Classical High's motto is a fitting one for the uncompromising literary theorist himself: "To Strive, to Seek, to Find, and Not to Yield."

Stanley and his classmates studied, as part of the curriculum, four years of Latin, as well as French and German. Having a facility with these three languages would give him a distinct advantage later in graduate school: he was able to take and pass all three language exams before he even started his studies. Classical High prided itself on a first-rate teaching staff. Whether it was physics, chemistry, trigonometry, or geometry, the instruction was of the highest caliber. Many of the teachers were women who had never married and who had devoted their lives to teaching. They were demanding. And patient. Their students were their lives. One in particular stood out to Stanley: Miss Sarah Flanagan, an English teacher. Her classes were inspiring and thought provoking; she was strict and somewhat aloof. She was the mentor who first pointed out to Stanley that he had a talent for writing and for thinking about poetry. Her encouragement made him begin to consider English as a potential area of study that he might pursue in college.

For several years, he thought he would become an architect. There were always architects—friends of Max—hanging around the Fish home. Among them was Percival Goodman, the famous urban architect who specialized in designing synagogues and other Jewish-oriented structures and brother of Paul Goodman, the prominent sociologist, poet, and intellectual. The young Stanley was inspired by these colorful characters and felt that he too could design buildings for a living. Max—half serious, half tongue in cheek—would inveigh against architects in a way that foreshadowed the theory/practice debates that Stanley would one day play such a central role in. "You architects don't seem to realize that water flows down, not up," he would say to his friends, by which he meant that architects may have ample book knowledge but often lack an understanding of how things actually work in the real world.

Stanley finally realized that his inability to draw well would be an insurmountable obstacle to his becoming an architect. Someone with mediocre drawing skills might well become a draftsman in the age of computers, but not before. So, ironically, Stanley chose to pursue English studies not because of an abiding love for writing and reading but because he would not be able to pursue architecture and because his teachers were pointing out that he had a genuine talent for writing and literary interpretation.

He would become the first in his extended family to attend college, after he graduated from high school in 1955. He had earned good grades (B plusses, mostly) at Classical High—not great grades, but good enough to make him competitive at a number of the nation's finest colleges. His SAT scores were good, too, but not impressive. He applied to only five schools—which, of course, was risky given the quality of colleges he applied to: Amherst, Brown, Columbia, Harvard, and Penn. He did not get into Columbia or Harvard and was placed on the waiting list at Amherst, his first choice, but he was quickly admitted to Brown and Penn.

He desperately wanted to attend Amherst because he had fallen in love with the college when he had taken a school-sponsored trip to visit colleges in the area. And then one of his friends—who had been class president, state rifle champ, and voted the most likely to succeed—applied to Amherst at the last minute and was immediately admitted. The writing was on the wall: given the nationwide competition for admission, Amherst was unlikely to admit more than one person from a small high school in Providence. So, although he had made the waiting list, he in the end was not accepted. That left Brown and Penn. The more he thought about it, the more he realized that he did not want to stay in Providence to attend Brown. His mother was driving him crazy, and he needed a change. He needed to strike out on his own, make his own life. That left Penn. And besides, his buddies would be going to Penn: Donny Dwares, Billy Meyers, and his special friend Bobby Roy, the all-star athlete who lived three houses down the street from him.

He may have been admitted to only two of his five choices, but this was still an impressive showing for a working-class boy who made respectable but not outstanding grades and who did not have the advantage—as did so many middle-class kids—of a family tradition of attending college. Those families had the advantage of knowing how colleges work, which ones are better than others, and which are more likely to admit you than not. Lacking this knowledge, many working-class kids don't know the difference between a Penn and a Penn State or the four-year college down the street and Amherst.

What made the difference in Stanley's case was the Jewish community of upwardly mobile families that he belonged to. Everyone helped one another; they pooled their knowledge and served as a large supportive family. In many ways this is a much more effective support network than simply one family would be—more input, advice, and knowledge is available to help you make your decisions. Stanley clearly benefited from this network.

After Stanley first applied to the five universities and before he began to hear from them, he suffered through a period of anxiety and doubt. He knew his grades and SAT scores were not as high as they could have been. And he also worried about another part of his record: he had twice been suspended from high school for disciplinary reasons. Early in his time at Classical he amused himself one Saturday morning by throwing rocks through the windows of the school building—and got caught. School officials summoned his parents to a meeting. Ever the rhetorician, Stanley convinced his parents that they did not need to attend the meeting; he would simply attend for them. He knew that Max would have been furious had he learned that his son was guilty of vandalism.

Stanley was suspended from school for a week. Shortly thereafter, one of his classmates, Jimmy Flynn, stole a car for a brief joy ride and was brought to the principal's office with his parents and a police officer. The principal was reported to have said to Jimmy's parents, "Do you want your son to become another Stanley Fish?"

On another occasion school officials caught Stanley running a sports gambling pool out of the school library. One of his peers who had been excluded from the pool had informed on him to the principal. Again he was suspended. Whether or not these incidents played a role in the decisions of Amherst, Columbia, and Harvard, no one knows, but the fact that Brown and Penn came through in the end was a great relief to young Stanley Fish.

Chapter 2

Escape from Providence:
The College Years

S tanley was almost gleeful that hot and humid summer of 1955 as he packed his bags to leave to attend the University of Pennsylvania. He realized how fortunate he was: he had gotten into a well-respected Ivy League college despite his record as a troublemaker and his less-than-outstanding grades. Almost as important: he would finally have a respite from his mother and the daily contentiousness of the Fish household. He would also have the good fortune of not being completely alone in a new town; he would enjoy the companionship of a few of his close neighborhood friends who would also be attending Penn. Yes, things couldn't have been better, he thought to himself.

Once on campus, he and his Providence pals all joined Alpha Epsilon Pi, a Jewish fraternity, and they even lived in the fraternity house during their sophomore and junior years. He found that he loved fraternity life. This new social network replaced the close network that he had enjoyed in the tight-knit Jewish community in his neighborhood back in Providence. He made many friends, and he continued his lifestyle essentially the way he had in Providence: in his spare time, he gambled, played basketball with his friends, and lusted after women. He had learned his lesson: no more pranks, no more tossing rocks through windows. He had matured considerably. While some of his fraternity brothers indulged in typical college-life pranks, he would have none of it. He would manage to survive the four years of college without getting into trouble once.

During his first year at Penn, he lived in a college residence hall. After he had been there a month or two and had developed a good rapport with his neighbors, his roommate and some of his friends in nearby suites decided an intervention was necessary: one sunny afternoon they escorted him on a tour of their closets so that he could learn what tasteful clothes looked like as opposed to the unfashionable working-class clothes that he usually wore. He shrugged and, a little red faced, said to his friends, "What do I know about clothes?" "Not much, that's for sure," his roommate shot back. Despite the teasing, Stanley appreciated his friends' advice, and he began to pay more attention to how he dressed—besides, he thought to himself, dressing fashionably might help him on the all-important dating scene.

Stanley quickly gained a reputation as a ladies' man. During his high school days he had dated two sisters, the Ettlinger twins, and they both ended up at Penn and became part of the Providence circle. Although he dated many women, he yearned for one in particular: Toby Eisenberg. She was smart, beautiful, and articulate—a perfect match for Stanley. They dated, he wooed her, he pampered her, he took her to the prom, but he never won her over completely. This was a great disappointment to him.

Always the entrepreneur (some would say, always on the make), Stanley decided that even though he was a freshman, he would run in the election for student-government offices. He chose the position of class secretary, primarily because the post entailed few responsibilities. He chose as his campaign manager a smart, industrious, and congenial friend of his who lived in the same hall: Jon Huntsman, the very Jon Huntsman who would become a billionaire and then father of the Jon Huntsman who would become governor of Utah and who would later run unsuccessfully for president of the United States. This was a wise choice on Stanley's part. He easily won. Barely a month or so at college and he was already making his mark.

As a college student he became much more serious about his studies. He had been a good student in high school, but not the best that he could have been. That would change now. He enjoyed his class work, but he found it to be exceedingly easy. Classical High School was much harder, he thought. Much of the material in his college classes he had already covered in classes at Classical; nonetheless, he always made sure that he was in command of whatever material was being studied. He did well, leaving ample time for all his extracurricular pursuits. For the rest of his life he would feel an intense loyalty to Classical High School. He could see how well that institution, with its devoted teachers, had prepared him academically. He would never feel that same loyalty for Penn—or for Yale, the other Ivy League school he would attend. Decades later, he would make donations to Classical, but not to Penn or Yale, and in April of 2015 Classical High would confer on him its prestigious "distinguished alumni award."

As a sophomore, he joined the student newspaper, the *Daily Pennsylvanian*, where he served as a reporter and where he continued to hone his entrepreneurial nature. During the 1956 campaign for the U.S. presidency, when Adlai Stevenson was running against Dwight D. Eisenhower for the second time, Stevenson gave a speech on campus. Stanley was the reporter assigned to cover the talk. Stevenson gave a wide-ranging talk covering many important points about domestic and foreign policy, but in one short sentence he seemed to slight former president Harry Truman. Stanley's journalistic instinct kicked in, and he made the slight the centerpiece of the story. This in turn drew complaints from several readers who felt that the attention to the slight eclipsed the substantive points that Stevenson had made, but the young reporter had done his job: he had reported what was newsworthy—after all, the venerable *Daily Pennsylvanian* was a respected newspaper, not a public-relations organ. Nor was Stanley a stranger to the newspaper business. During high school he had joined Junior Achievement, the organization that attempts to introduce youngsters to the business world by arranging for them to take on real-world business ventures, albeit on a small scale. Stanley had chosen as his project to create and operate a local newspaper. He had done such a good job with this venture that he had been chosen to attend the national Junior Achievement convention.

Before beginning his senior year Stanley moved out of the Alpha Epsilon Pi fraternity house and rented a small, two-bedroom apartment with three friends from Penn. They would throw many parties that year in the apartment. One of his flatmates, Mitchel Craner, was from New Rochelle, a small city in nearby southeastern New York. Early in the school year, Mitchel threw a party and invited a number of his hometown friends. Among them was Adrienne Aaron, a smart, vivacious Jewish woman with an acerbic wit. Like Stanley, she was articulate and strong willed—some would say too strong willed. They were immediately attracted to one another. Although Adrienne had come to the party with a date, she and Stanley spent much time that evening getting to know one another, and they made plans to continue to do so in the near future. Adrienne had been a student at the University of Michigan but had transferred to Boston University to pursue a romance that ultimately fizzled. She had recently graduated from Boston University. This budding relationship would eventually evolve into a romance, a proposal, and a wedding.

The professors at Penn who had the greatest influence on Stanley professionally were two scholars of eighteenth-century British literature: Maurice Johnson and Arthur H. Scouten. Johnson had written books on the works of Jonathan Swift; Scouten was a scholar of Restoration and eighteenth-century English drama. Both were inspiring teachers. Stanley was fascinated by Scouten. He was a lively, colorful character from Louisiana with a distinct southern drawl, and before joining the academy he had worked as Huey Long's personal chauffeur. Long's code name for him was "Joe." Arthur was quite a character; he would mesmerize people with his tales of the old days with the Kingfish. These two scholars showed Stanley a whole new side of the academic life: they were players—they published books and articles, they were prominent in their fields, they influenced how other scholars think, they were respected. He began to think that perhaps one day he too could be a player, that one day he too could write books and influence how other scholars think, that one day he would be universally respected.

When Stanley visited Johnson's office for the first time, he was in awe; he had never seen an entire book-lined wall before. Book-lined walls were common in professors' offices, but this was a first for Stanley. He had become accustomed to visiting his aunt and uncle in the flat downstairs and perusing their modest library of popular classics, but entire walls tightly packed with substantial and important books—this was a vision. And when Johnson told the naïve freshman that he also had walls full of books in his home, Stanley was flabbergasted. This one vision, this one mental snapshot of a scholar's den with walls full of books, had a major effect on him. He was hooked. This was his life. He could taste it. He wanted it. He would get it.

He was drawn both to their forceful personalities and to the literature they were teaching. They both had very different personalities. Johnson was patrician and well connected in upper-class Philadelphia society. He was a precise person with a dry and rapier wit. He was aloof and always seemed to exude a mild disdain for anyone he addressed.

Scouten, in contrast, was a character, some odd combination of Li'l Abner, Dr. Johnson, and Juvenal. He was a master of satire and seemed to see the world always through a satiric lens, which was the source of great entertainment to those around him. These two powerful and very different personalities were formative for the beginning English major. They taught him a love of eighteenth-century literature. He was drawn to its neoclassical rationality and conservatism. He liked the Swiftian satiric persona, the biting irony; he liked Pope's neatly crafted couplets, their precision. He felt very much at home in the eighteenth century.

Of course, other professors influenced him as well. One was Clyde Ryals, a scholar of British Victorian literature and the world's foremost authority on the Scottish author Thomas Carlyle (and later a colleague of his at Duke). Another was Morse Peckham, a brilliant and distinguished professor of comparative literature. Peckham was famous for demonstrating how various arts in a given age—poetry, opera, music, painting—all illustrated a similar aesthetic sensibility and philosophical understanding of the world. Stanley took a course from him and felt that Peckham was brilliant in ways that he could never have been, but at the same time he was skeptical of this comparativist approach; he felt much more comfortable in the realm of close readings of texts. Later in his career he would read Meyer Abrams's *The Mirror and the Lamp*, which is also a philosophical, theoretical work about artistic sensibilities; he would find it to be an extraordinary piece of work and persuasive in ways that Peckham's was not.

These were exceedingly powerful role models for the young English major. He was learning from some of the most accomplished and influential literary scholars of the time. Both Johnson and Scouten recognized that Stanley had an unusual talent for literary interpretation, and they urged him to apply to graduate school; they knew that he had the potential to become a player—just like them. It was in part through their efforts that he would later be admitted to Yale. In those days, Yale was reluctant to admit Penn graduates to their graduate programs. Given the institutional prejudices at the time, Elis were not likely to acknowledge that Penn was in fact a legitimate member of the prestigious Ivy League. When Fish applied for admission to graduate school at Yale in the spring of 1959, the English department had not admitted a Penn graduate for many years. When they finally admitted Stanley, some said condescendingly that it was a kind of experiment: they wanted to see if a Penn graduate could survive Yale's rigorous curriculum.

He had applied to several graduate programs in English, and he had even taken the Law School Admission Test (LSAT), thinking that he might attend law school. He was surprised to find that he had scored higher on the LSAT than he had on the Graduate Record Examination. Indiana University swiftly admitted him to the graduate program in English and offered a scholarship. He had applied to Indiana at the urging of a professor there named Roy Smalley. Stanley had taken a course in Victorian literature from him during the summer of his junior year when he attended summer school at Harvard University. He went there to continue his study of Latin, and he picked up some Greek as well. Smalley was there to teach for the summer, so Stanley enrolled in his course for fun. Smalley had two favorite students that summer whose papers he would ask to be read aloud to the class. One was Stanley; the other was Adrienne Rich. Stanley was fascinated by the soon-to-be-famous feminist poet and essayist, so he asked her out. She stared at him for a long moment and then politely declined. The Indiana offer was attractive; the scholarship was generous. Then Yale came through. He had a very difficult decision to make. Yale was offering modest assistance, and the law schools were offering none. He agonized over the choice. He first ruled out law school; he needed to have some assistance. Financially, he would be much better off at Indiana. But who turns down Yale? In the end, he chose Yale.

His relationship with Adrienne Aaron had gotten quite serious. He proposed to her; she accepted. The couple was very excited about the future. Cosmopolitan at heart, Adrienne was very much against a move to Indiana, and this became part of the decision to go to Yale. For that matter, she was not wild about moving to a small, boring city in Connecticut either, although at least it was on the East Coast, not far from civilization. In fact, it would not become clear to Stanley until after moving to Yale, but both Adrienne and her mother were skeptical about the viability of a career as an English professor. They were an upper-middle-class family from fashionable New Rochelle—a career in law was one thing, but a career as a poorly paid professor seemed a dead end, a strategic cul-de-sac. Both secretly hoped he would soon abandon this frivolous course and switch to a more lucrative profession. But this would only emerge as a point of contention in a year or so. For the moment, Adrienne and Stanley were very happy and were excited about beginning their life together. They were married in a formal ceremony by Rabbi Eli Bohnen on Sunday, August 23, 1959.

The wedding took place in New York City in the luxurious Essex House Hotel across the street from Central Park. The towering forty-four-story art deco hotel was the perfect setting for their large and opulent wedding. The couple stood proudly under the elaborately adorned huppah and happily received Rabbi Bohnen's blessings. They exchanged rings—and a kiss—and then, following Jewish tradition, Stanley, with one swift stomp of his right foot, smashed to smithereens a wine glass wrapped in a fine linen cloth, a ritual meant to remind those in attendance, even on this day of great joy, of the hardships suffered by the Jewish people.

The reception was a lavish affair full of excess and overindulgence, a feast of sumptuous food and drink. Elegant linen-draped tables displayed platters of spicy roast chicken and lamb, bowls of rice pilaf and roasted vegetables, serving pans of rich kugel and potato latkes, not to mention basket upon basket of freshly baked challah. A large dessert table featured platters of fresh-baked mandelbrot, bowls of fresh fruit and sour cream, a variety of luscious cakes, and platters of exotic tortes. Of course, there was champagne, an endless supply of it. And there was dancing—endless dancing! The couple would then honeymoon on the island of Saint Croix in the U.S. Virgin Islands.

That summer, the couple traveled to New Haven and rented an attractive apartment not far from the Yale campus. They immediately began to develop a close circle of friends.

During the orientation of new students, one of his classmates, Richard Lanham, who would later become a famous author and scholar himself, was standing behind him in line with other incoming graduate students, waiting to be processed and made official. Many of their colleagues-to-be were preening and making every attempt to impress everybody else with their sophistication. One carried a copy of *War and Peace* under his arm; another was scanning a copy of the *Times Literary Supplement*; others carried similarly weighty works obviously displayed for all to see. Stanley, who was perusing the sporting news, suddenly wheeled around and without introduction said, "Boy, I wish I had a piece of Sonny Liston." An avid sports fan, Stanley had rightly judged that Liston was well on his way to becoming heavyweight boxing champion. Lanham didn't know who Sonny Liston was or what it meant to have a piece of him, but he was immediately impressed by Stanley's genuineness and lack of pretention. They introduced themselves and became lifelong friends.

Like many of his peers, Lanham perceived Stanley to be mature and shrewd and to have a clear understanding of the professional life he was joining. He felt that Stanley seemed to get the rules of the game down right away, whereas he had to struggle to figure out how things work. He could not have been more wrong—on both points.

While Stanley had found Penn to be enjoyable and quite easy, his first year at Yale was extremely difficult. The work was grueling and the atmosphere was very competitive, not at all warm or friendly. He had yet to develop a sense of how the profession works, while many of his fellow students at Yale already had. Maurice Johnson and Arthur Scouten had been exceptionally supportive of Stanley and had helped him get into Yale, but they had not mentored him about the profession. As a result, he felt totally out to sea and out of place. He was plagued by self-doubt. Perhaps he did not belong in graduate school after all. He often thought of quitting graduate school altogether. That first semester he took four classes, two of which were on Friday. Every Friday evening for the first few months, after attending his week of courses, he would resolve to quit graduate school; by the next Tuesday he would convince himself to give it another try. Eventually he got the hang of it, but he realized that if he was to be successful, to become a real player, he had substantial catch-up work to do.

He was driven. He knew he was behind his fellow graduate students in knowledge and preparation. He decided he would spend the entire next summer reading intensively. Adrienne worked as an editorial assistant for the well-known psychologist John Dollard, author of the acclaimed *Caste and Class in a Southern Town*, so she was earning enough money to support them that summer of 1960. Stanley had a part-time job as a clerk on weekends and two nights a week in a drugstore in nearby Hamden, Connecticut, so he had substantial blocks of free time; he would devote as much of it as possible to get up to speed. Every day he would go to the Linonia and Brothers Reading Room in Yale's Sterling

Memorial Library, which in those days was a males-only room, and he would read every important primary work of literature he could. He read many Jacobean plays and pages upon pages of poetry. He concentrated on works that he had not read previously. That summer he read *Paradise Lost* five times. As a result of this intensive immersion in the literature, he felt more at ease when he returned in the fall semester of his second year. He had regained his characteristic self-confidence and swagger.

He would maintain this same work ethic not only during his remaining Yale years but throughout his entire life. He was single-mindedly hardworking. Each morning, Adrienne would prepare a lunch for him, which he would take in a little brown paper bag to the library, where he would work without interruption. Unlike many of his colleagues, who liked to indulge in long, leisurely lunches at the local sandwich shops, Stanley felt that this was inefficient, a terrible waste of precious time. Instead, he would munch on his sandwiches while reading and scrawling paragraphs in his notebook. He even maintained this working-lunch ethic decades later when he was a dean. Most deans use every lunch hour to court potential donors or conduct some type of official business. Not Stanley. These hours were too valuable. In fact, he made use of every bit of available time. If he was in the train station and had ten minutes before his train arrived, he would pull out his notebook and resume the paragraph that he had been writing. He was a master of time management.

Stanley immediately stood out at Yale—in ways that would begin the legend of his being academe's enfant terrible. Yale graduate school had a reputation of being a bit stuffy and staid. Faculty and graduate students did not dress flamboyantly or drive fancy cars. Several prided themselves on driving Volkswagens and Volvos. Stanley arrived at Yale driving a shiny new Mercedes-Benz. Several faculty raised eyebrows and began to talk among themselves about the new upstart who dared show up with a luxury car. Perhaps he wasn't a serious scholar after all. Hearing the gossip, Stanley sold the Mercedes and replaced it with a Porsche, further scandalizing them. From the beginning, he did not feel that he had to pretend, as so many academics tend to do, to take a vow of poverty in order to be a legitimate scholar. In fact, he vowed to himself then that he would one day become the highest-paid English professor in the nation—which essentially meant in the entire world. He would achieve that goal.

He had great admiration for several of his fellow students: they were bright, sophisticated, and well read. One in particular, Michael O'Loughlin, seemed a natural at advanced academic work. He never seemed to struggle, in the same way that Stanley never struggled as an undergraduate. O'Loughlin was a true intellectual, someone who lived the life of the mind. The academic life—a life of books and ideas (and in many languages)—was natural to him. That's what he did. Even after a hugely successful career as an academic and a public intellectual, Stanley never thought of himself as an intellectual. Academic work was something he liked to do and that he excelled at, but he saw it more as a job than a calling. When he was "off the clock," you would not find him relaxing on the couch, reading a Portuguese epic in Portuguese, which is exactly what O'Loughlin would likely be doing. He would later think of Harold Bloom, Geoffrey Hartman, and Richard Rorty as true intellectuals, but not himself.

Stanley studied literary criticism under the legendary William Wimsatt. As a teacher, Wimsatt was stern and fierce, and his courses were rigorous and grueling—much like those depicted in *The Paper Chase*. He was a tall man, almost seven feet tall, with a fierce demeanor. He would say things like, "Some of my colleagues believe that I'm too combative and polemical in my critical stances," and then he would go on to suggest that there was something very important at stake in the work they were doing in class so they had better take it seriously. Of all the courses Stanley took in graduate school, the conceptually abstract level at which Wimsatt posed questions was remarkable and unmatched. Most of his other professors were also brilliant scholars with extensive accomplishments, but as far as thinking through interpretive, philosophical issues, no one could match Wimsatt. This was a talent Stanley himself would cultivate throughout his career.

During the semester that Stanley was taking Wimsatt's course in literary theory, Adrienne and Stanley took one of their frequent trips into New York City—to civilization. They were tooling around a Barnes and Noble, when suddenly Stanley stumbled upon a book, *A Short History of Literary Criticism*, by none other than Wimsatt and Cleanth Brooks. He had not known of this book and was shocked to find it on the shelf. He took it back to New Haven as a trophy and proudly boasted to his colleagues about his find, only to discover that they all had the book!

As it turned out, although Wimsatt had not assigned the text, his course followed the text closely; he was teaching the course from his own book. Needless to say, Stanley found the second half of the semester much easier than the first now that he had the inside information that everyone else seemed to have.

Wimsatt was the object of great admiration and the subject of a fair amount of amusement among faculty and staff. At nearly seven feet tall, he towered over everyone. During the semester that Stanley took Wimsatt's course, he was so amused by Wimsatt's physical stature that he encouraged Adrienne to come to the classroom building before class one day, saying, "You've got to see this guy. You won't believe it!" She came before the class started, and the couple stationed themselves at one end of a long hallway. The double doors at the other end suddenly opened and there, backlit, stood a larger-than-life figure, who paused briefly and then started striding toward them. It was quite a sight. Adrienne gasped.

That semester, one of the students was a Catholic nun. One evening, Wimsatt discovered that the nun did not have a ride home from class and was planning to walk. The class was held from four to six on Friday afternoons, and by six it was already dark out. A committed Roman Catholic, Wimsatt did not want a nun walking home on a dark Friday evening in New Haven, so he offered to drive her home. He invited Stanley to come along. When they got to the car, Stanley noticed something strange. At first he could not figure out what was wrong, and then he finally realized what it was: because Wimsatt was such a tall man with long legs and the car was so small, he had removed the driver's seat and drove from the backseat—another sight to be seen.

Wimsatt was a central proponent of what became known as the New Criticism, as was his colleague Cleanth Brooks, author of the seminal *The Well Wrought Urn*. Both were titans in English studies at the time. Stanley served as Brooks's teaching assistant for one year, helping to teach a course in Romantic poetry. In the middle of the semester, Brooks became ill, and Stanley was tasked with teaching the course for a few weeks. Stanley discovered that he liked Romantic poetry despite the fact that it was a reaction against the Augustan poetry that he so admired. Over the years, he and his fellow graduate students found great amusement in watching Brooks and Wimsatt stroll down the hallway together —the imposing Wimsatt towering over Brooks, the short, soft-spoken southern gentleman. They seemed like the academic equivalent of Laurel and Hardy.

Wimsatt's course in literary criticism was formative to the budding scholar, and so too was a course taught by Helge Kökeritz, a Danish philologist and expert in the history of the English language. Kökeritz was famous for his research into how the English of Chaucer and Shakespeare was pronounced. Stanley, along with his classmate Richard Lanham, took a class with Kökeritz and as a result became interested in and knowledgeable about classical, medieval, and Renaissance rhetoric.

In terms of critical reading, the course that probably influenced Stanley the most was one taught by John Pope, a noted scholar of Anglo-Saxon poetic meter. Pope was a Spenserian, and Stanley took his course in Spenser's works. He also studied Victorian poetry under Dwight Culler, a very rigorous old-style scholar and father of literary theorist Jonathan Culler, and he studied sixteenth-century literature with Richard (Dick) Sylvester, a specialist in the works of Sir Thomas More.

Perhaps Stanley's greatest disappointment arose from a course in eighteenth-century literature that he took from Martin Price. A student of Maynard Mack, Price was considered one on the twentieth-century's most eminent scholars of Augustan literature. Understandably, Stanley assumed that he would specialize in eighteenth-century literature, given the tutelage of Johnson and Scouten back at Penn, but one course from Price convinced him that he had no talent for the eighteenth century. He did not do well.

Of this star-studded coterie of scholars, perhaps the most eminent was the professor who would become Stanley's dissertation director, E. Talbot Donaldson, one of the greatest Chaucerians of his generation. As a teacher, Donaldson was always funny and had a sardonic wit. Stanley, perhaps unconsciously, would adopt a teaching style very similar to Donaldson's. Following Donaldson, the cornerstone of Stanley's teaching is humor. Either in a stand-up lecture setting or a traditional classroom, he is funny and entertaining. Good teaching for Stanley is a performance. He came to believe that effective teaching is a function of one's personality and that certain kinds of teaching styles are not available to you given the limitations, strengths, and weaknesses of your personality. That being said, he runs a very tight ship in the classroom. He informs students in their very first class session that he is not interested whatsoever in their personal opinion about anything they are studying. Their job is to master the material, not offer impressions prior to earning the right to express them. Of course, he delivers this dictum in a kind of self-mocking, quasi-dictatorial tone, so he is able to keep control of the classroom while being an entertaining performer. This teaching style, which he honed over many decades, owes much to Donaldson's good example set back in the early 1960s.

Among the eminent scholars at Yale in those days was a group of assistant professors who would one day become as prominent, but they weren't allowed to teach graduate students, so Stanley got to know them socially when he played second base on the Yale English department softball team. There was E. D. Hirsch, the originator of the concept of "cultural literacy"; Harry Berger Jr., a prolific Renaissance and Shakespeare scholar; Harry Schroeder, the Chaucerian; and Harold Bloom, who would become a megastar in the academic firmament. Stanley would develop relationships with these academic heavyweights, his future colleagues on the national scene. Clearly, the Yale English department at that time was a rich intellectual environment and the perfect training for someone to shake up the intellectual world, as Stanley would in due time.

In those days the Yale English department offered an experimental program in which students could earn a PhD in three years. Students did not produce a master's thesis; they progressed directly through to the dissertation. Stanley and some of his colleagues opted for the three-year degree. He thought to himself that graduate school is not a natural existence, and living in New Haven is certainly not a natural existence (at least to him), either, so the sooner he could leave Yale the better. Adrienne, of course, was quick to agree.

At first he was planning to write a dissertation on the works of Lord Byron. He had taken a course in Romantic poetry from Frederick Pottle, perhaps the world's foremost Boswell scholar but also a respected analyst of Romantic poetry. Stanley wrote his final paper on Byron's *Don Juan*, which he conceived as really more neoclassical than Romantic. This paper was so successful and well received that he thought he would write a dissertation on the subject. There was only one obstacle, however: one of his peers had already declared that she would write a dissertation on Byron, and it was a custom in the department that no two dissertators would compete with one another by writing dissertations on a similar subject. It was up to the two dissertators to sort it out. Stanley could see that his colleague had an extraordinary investment in Byron scholarship, whereas he was only pursuing the subject for fun, so he volunteered not to write on Byron.

He then had to decide what to write on. When he had taken a course in sixteenth-century literature with Dick Sylvester, he found that he was drawn to the works of John Skelton. To Stanley, Skelton seemed agreeably odd and, indeed, somewhat insane. And his was a manageable corpus. Stanley was already well read in the era, so he decided that he would become an early Renaissance or late medieval-period specialist. (And, in fact, that is what he would be for the first five or six years of his teaching career.) There was very little secondary work on Skelton at the time. A few scholars were writing on Skelton; there was some work on Malory; and there was some work on the Scottish Chaucerians. There was very little work on the big literary figures, like John Lydgate, although Stanley's future colleague at Berkeley, Alain Renoir, would write a book on Lydgate, saying that he did so because Lydgate was the dullest person in the world and he wanted to write a book on him. So, Stanley deemed Skelton's works to be an interestingly uncharted field. He set out to write his dissertation on Skelton. This was a purely opportunistic decision. It's not that he had fallen in love with the work. He found it interesting and funny, and it presented some problems in intellectual history that he found challenging.

Skelton was a Catholic poet living at a time when England was clearly turning away from Catholicism. His principal enemy—who was not a good enemy to have—was Cardinal Thomas Wolsey, one of the most powerful people in all of England. Unafraid, Skelton wrote biting satires on the court and Wolsey himself, such as "Speke, Parrot" (one of Stanley's favorites) and "Why Come Ye Nat to Courte?," which in certain ways anticipates John Donne's satires.

Stanley asked the eminent Talbot Donaldson to serve as his major professor, and he agreed, saying, "Okay, do your dissertation on Skelton, but if you're going to get anywhere in the profession, you are going to have to write scholarship on a major figure, as well." Skelton was not considered a major poet; he was more of an important minor poet. Donaldson was a good dissertation advisor for Stanley: he left him alone to do his work. Stanley wrote his dissertation, "The Poetry of Awareness: A

Reassessment of John Skelton," quite quickly. He completed his degree in January of 1962 and immediately turned his attention to the search for a suitable academic appointment.

While Stanley had many friends among the Yale graduate students, a smaller inner circle was especially tight-knit. At its core were Richard Lanham, the future rhetoric scholar who first met Stanley in line during the orientation process for new students; Michael O'Loughlin, the student who impressed Stanley as the true intellectual among the group; and Bart Giamatti, a student of Renaissance literature who would go on to become the president of Yale and then the commissioner of Major League Baseball. It also included Rachel Meyer, George Farr (who went on to become a high-ranking official at the National Endowment for the Humanities, including briefly serving as its deputy chairman), and Judy Banzer. A favorite of everyone was Marion Van Horn. She was the belle, the one that everyone was in love with, especially Michael O'Loughlin. He seemed to fantasize about her every minute of the day.

Socially, Adrienne and Stanley attended and threw many parties for the graduate students and faculty during their years at Yale. They were gracious hosts and sought-after guests. While Adrienne was liked by many of her husband's colleagues, she remained an intimidating personality to some. She was an outspoken, opinionated, high-energy dynamo whose very presence "terrified" some of the female graduate students and intellectually and socially "threatened" the males. She had a very sharp tongue and sarcastic turn of mind. Some thought of her as the consummate snob in all matters of taste—art, clothes, food, wine. The rumor was that she belonged to an Ayn Rand cell, and although the rumor was untrue (she was a down-the-line northeastern liberal Democrat), it further fueled her status as someone to be wary of. One thing was certain: the couple always added zest to any gathering.

Stanley gained a reputation among his peers not only for his shrewdness and tough-mindedness, but also for his kindness and sensitivity to those around him. He would be the first to congratulate a colleague who had just received news of some good fortune—a publication acceptance or a teaching award—and he was known to be exceedingly polite.

At home and increasingly more in public, the couple continued to bicker with one another. Some saw these bouts as a kind of "shtick" they performed; others were put off by the discord. Stanley himself began to dislike the confrontational rut they had fallen into. He began to liken his marriage to his relationship with his mother: incessant arguing and jockeying for position. Nevertheless, these years were full of good times and excitement, especially as they anticipated what their future would offer once Stanley found an academic appointment.

One sunny spring day in 1962, after Stanley had finished playing an especially grueling game of basketball in the Yale gym, he decided to stop by the English department to see if he had any mail. Who knows? he thought. There might be some good news about his job search. He tried to slip into the department surreptitiously because he was dressed in shorts, tattered sneakers, and a sopping wet tee shirt and did not want to be seen by any of his colleagues—especially his professors. The department secretary, however, caught a glimpse of him out of the corner of her eye as he ducked into the mail room. "Mr. Fish, the chairman would like to speak with you," she announced imperiously. "He is available right now." The chairman was Frederick W. Hilles, a distinguished eighteenth-century scholar. Despite his disheveled and redolent attire, Stanley sauntered tentatively into the chair's office, wondering if he was in trouble for some reason. "Mr. Fish," Hilles said in his usual commanding voice, "Ron Paulson is leaving the University of Illinois to take a position at Rice." He paused. Stanley frantically tried to determine the significance of this announcement. Who's Ron Paulson to me? I don't really know Paulson, he thought. Paulson had graduated from Yale in 1958 with a PhD in English and had accepted a position first as an instructor and then as an assistant professor at the University of Illinois. He would later become a colleague of Stanley's at Johns Hopkins University and a close friend. Stanley certainly had no interest at the moment in the movement and progress of Paulson's academic career. "What is this guy trying to tell me?" he asked himself. The chair continued: "That means a slot at Illinois is now open, and we think that you would be the ideal person to fill it."

Stanley was astonished. He had heard rumors among the graduate students that this is how the old boys' network worked in academe. In those days, before a strong sense of shared governance (which would only begin to develop later in that decade) and equal opportunity guidelines (which would be established much later), department chairs and influential senior professors were power brokers. Prestigious institutions such as Yale could expect "slots" at other universities that could be filled by someone at Yale telephoning the appropriate person at a given university and saying, "You have a vacancy in British Romantic poetry, so we'd like to send you so-and-so." Often no formal search was conducted, just a gentlemen's handshake—and in those days, it was mostly men doing the handshaking; relatively few women populated the professoriate. So, undoubtedly when Paulson announced that he was vacating his position at the University of Illinois, Maynard Mack and a few of the more influential professors in the department sat down together (perhaps with glasses of scotch in front of them, which was not uncommon in those days) and asked one another, "Well, what are we going to do with our Illinois slot?" Someone in the room likely replied, "Perhaps Fish would be a good candidate. Let's see how faculty in Urbana, Illinois, take to young professors who drive Porsches."

Stanley was a bit taken aback by the chair's offer, and he promised to give it careful consideration. When he got home, he immediately told Adrienne about the unexpected opportunity. She stared at him for a long moment without saying anything, and he thought he detected daggers in her eyes. He had dragged her to New Haven, and now he was proposing to drag her to the cornfields of the Midwest. In an unusually quiet voice, she told him of a friend of hers who had been engaged to a medical student at Columbia, who one day announced to her friend that when his residency was complete he planned to practice medicine in his hometown, Cincinnati. Adrienne paused for an interminable moment, and then said simply, "He went alone to Cincinnati." Stanley got the message. He was not even certain where Illinois was. His sense of geography had always been abysmal. Given Adrienne's vehemence, he was glad that he had thought to run the offer by her first.

Soon after politely declining the Illinois arrangement, Stanley received an offer from the University of Wisconsin. He had interviewed with the famed Helen C. White, a scholar of medieval and Renaissance literature and one of the few women in the professoriate in those days. An imposing figure, she was chair of the department at the time. She would go on to become president of the American Association of University Women and a recipient of the Order of the British Empire, an honor conferred by Queen Elizabeth II of Great Britain. The University of Wisconsin would honor her posthumously by naming a library building after her: Helen C. White Hall. The offer to Stanley entailed his appointment at the rank of instructor, and he would be expected to serve as an assistant to Professor White. She taught huge lecture classes, and new instructors would typically teach smaller sections of these students when she was not lecturing. This arrangement was unacceptable to Stanley. He had had a similar arrangement when he served as Cleanth Brooks's teaching assistant, and he could not envision becoming a player in the discipline by beginning from the type of position Wisconsin was offering. Besides, Adrienne was not keen on living in Madison. He declined the offer.

Adrienne and Stanley then experienced an agonizing period of anxiety. There were endless nights of nail biting and second-guessing. Perhaps we should have gone to Illinois, he thought. What's wrong with cornfields? Maybe we should have gone to Wisconsin. After all, it's a first-rate public university. They had turned down two sure bets, with no expectation that other offers would materialize. And then, unexpectedly and without ceremony, the University of California at Berkeley made him an offer. Geographically challenged, Stanley was not even certain where Berkeley was located; he just knew it was somewhere in California. Academic jobs were so plentiful in 1962 that departments often made offers to aspiring assistant professors on the basis of interviews at the Modern Language Association convention and telephone calls to their major professors—and without inviting the candidates for campus visits. This was the case with Berkeley. At that time, Berkeley's English department seemed to favor Harvard PhDs. It boasted only two notable Yale graduates: the prominent eighteenth-century and folklore scholar Bertrand H. Bronson, and the distinguished Chaucerian Charles Muscatine. Stanley would make it a trio.

Chapter 3

West of Everything:
The Berkeley Years

That summer of 1962 Adrienne and Stanley enthusiastically packed their pearly white Porsche and embarked on the long cross-country trip to the West Coast. They planned a leisurely route that would take them first to Ann Arbor, where Adrienne had attended college, and then to Madison, Wisconsin, just to see the campus they had turned down. When they arrived on the Wisconsin campus, Stanley was more certain than ever that they had made the right choice. That small college town would have suffocated them. And besides, it was a hotbed of liberalism, and he was not quite sure that he approved of that.

When they arrived in Berkeley, they checked into a motel and then started feverishly searching for an apartment. They eventually settled on the Mark Twain Apartments near campus. It was a new facility, and the two-bedroom, two-bath flat with a balcony overlooking College Avenue seemed quite a deal for a hundred dollars a month.

The weekend before the semester began and as everyone was settling into their new homes and offices, Adrienne and Stanley puzzled over what they should do with a large plush rug that they had shipped to California along with the rest of their belongings. The rug was originally a gift from a cousin of Stanley's who owned a carpet store. This large red—very red—carpet had adorned their living room in New Haven. They no longer had a use for the gift because the apartment they had rented came with newly installed wall-to-wall carpeting. Stanley snapped his fingers and said, "I know, I'll just take it to work and throw it in my office. It could use some carpeting." That Sunday afternoon he drove to his office and stretched the rug from his desk to the office door, covering the cold linoleum floor. There was a large gap between the floor and the bottom of the door, and the light hit the rug in such a way as to emit a rosy hue noticeable to everyone who happened to walk by in the hallway.

Stanley had yet to meet his officemate, Dorothy Finkelstein. She was the wife of a Judaic studies professor and was considerably older than the assistant professors. Many believed that she deserved a professorial appointment, but she had been forced to accept an appointment as a lecturer, instead. The next morning, when she reported to work and spied the rug and the rosy light emitting from the office, she turned red herself. "What potentate have they put in my office?" she said to any of her colleagues that she came upon that day. She was incensed. Another institutional slap in the face. This story immediately circulated throughout the department and was still being circulated nationally decades later. Of course, it became greatly embellished over time. The resulting narrative sounds something like this: this upstart assistant professor who drives a new Porsche and rents a stylish, modern apartment on College Avenue took one look at his department office and said, "This will never do." He proceeded to transform the nondescript office by installing plush carpeting, replacing the characterless institutional furniture with sleek modern pieces, and adorning the walls with attractive wall hangings. Stanley's reputation as a maverick—a future enfant terrible—was now firmly established, and it was only the first day of his first semester as a professional.

After the rug incident, Stanley would have an uneasy relationship with his officemate. Students would frequently visit him in the office to discuss their progress in his class or a draft of a paper. Academe had yet to develop a consciousness of gender politics as it related to the inherent power imbalance between professors and students, so flirting was an all-too-common practice. Dorothy would watch him with disdain as he tutored his female students. Finally, one afternoon after he had completed a number of student conferences, she turned to him and said scornfully, "The only thing worse than a lecher is a young lecher." Stanley smiled broadly.

Adrienne and Stanley settled into life at Berkeley with ease. They quickly made many friends and acclimated to Berkeley and the West Coast. It was a time of exuberance and high spirits.

After Stanley had been at Berkeley for only a few weeks, one of his colleagues, the Renaissance scholar Stephen Orgel, pulled him aside and said mischievously, "Before you came to campus, we all heard two things: that you had a four hundred horsepower car and a four thousand horsepower wife." Stanley replied forcefully, "Right—on both counts!"

By all accounts, Adrienne was a woman who knew her own mind; she was smart, ambitious, outspoken, always prepared to express herself, and decidedly not intimidated by her husband as so many of his colleagues were. She was short in stature, like her husband, and like her husband she made up for her shortness with a forceful personality. While she was not a warm person, and some called her "difficult," she nonetheless livened up every social situation she found herself in. She was fiercely loyal to and protective of Stanley. She would not tolerate anyone trying to criticize him, and she would quickly and vociferously give a piece of her mind to anyone who tried.

When Stanley first accepted the position at Berkeley, the annual salary was to be $4,800, but before he arrived on campus, the state legislature unexpectedly approved a salary increase for state employees, including university faculty, and so his starting salary was a whopping $5,100, a respectable salary at the time for an entry-level professor. He began at the rank of instructor with a course load of three courses each semester. That first semester he taught two sections of composition and a section of the first half of the British literature survey, Beowulf through the Eighteenth Century. After his first year he would be promoted to assistant professor and assigned an office of his own.

The 1960s were boom years for higher education. New colleges sprang up across the country seemingly overnight, and well-established colleges went on extended hiring sprees. It was a time of unchecked exuberance and expansion. The Berkeley English department hired six other entry-level professors along with Stanley that year. The next year they hired thirteen more. Among those hired with Stanley were scholars who would go on to become trendsetters in their disciplines: Stephen Booth, the accomplished Shakespearean who became Stanley's closest friend at Berkeley; Paul J. Alpers, the great Spenserian; Paul Alkon, the eighteenth-century specialist; George A. Starr, another eighteenth-century scholar who wrote acclaimed books on Daniel Defoe; Paul F. Theiner, an Old English and Medieval Latinist; and Gardner Stout, a scholar of the works of Laurence Sterne.

Booth and Stanley instantly became fast friends and ended up being assigned to the same suite of offices in the English department. Booth was witty and exceptionally smart—a well-loved colleague. Early after they first met, Stanley invited Booth to his apartment to socialize. Booth's wife hadn't yet arrived in town, so he was alone. Adrienne and Stanley wanted to help make him feel less isolated, and they planned a congenial evening in their stylish two-bedroom flat. Refusing to settle for the eclectic furnishings that one might typically find in the homes of young, struggling academics, Adrienne had furnished the entire apartment with beautiful Danish teak furniture with its clean, elegant lines and gleaming wood surfaces. She topped it off with exquisite designer quality lamps and elegant wall hangings. The apartment appeared to have been decorated by a professional. At the appointed time, Booth rang the bell, and Adrienne and Stanley greeted him warmly. He entered the apartment, stopped abruptly, looked from left to right, and then sadly shook his head, saying in a disapproving tone, "False values." Adrienne's jaw dropped. What was he saying? she thought. Are we required to take a vow of poverty just because Stan is a professor? She flashed a stern look at her guest, and then he winked at her impishly. They all laughed uproariously. Once the two scholars had become good friends, Stanley visited one of Booth's classes to make a presentation on Ben Jonson's "On My First Daughter." After the twenty-minute presentation, Booth looked at his students and said, "Don't worry. Twenty minutes after Dr. Fish leaves, the poem will snap back into shape." They all chuckled.

Intellectually, Stanley was especially close to Booth and to the Chomskyan linguist Julian C. Boyd, who had joined the Berkeley faculty in 1964. Booth was already attempting to transcend formalist approaches to literary texts by examining the text in relation to the reader, so his long discussions with Stanley were of great help to them both as they independently worked through the theoretical underpinnings of what would become known as Reader Response Criticism. And Boyd and Stanley would constantly play ideas off of one another, test hypotheses, and argue positions. This fertile intellectual banter was mutually beneficial to both scholars, and they remained in touch for decades until Boyd died in 2005. Stanley's intellectual relationships with these two scholars had a lasting effect on all three, although, curiously, he acknowledges neither in his original preface to *Surprised by Sin*. He instead recognizes Paul Alpers's "cogent criticisms" and George Starr's "advice and counsel." Starr reciprocated by dedicating his *Defoe and Casuistry* (1971) to Stanley,

Frederick Crews, and Julie Bader (who would later become his wife), not because any of the three had helped with the book but because he was proud to be at Berkeley and to have them as his colleagues.

While Stanley developed especially close relationships with Booth, Boyd, Alkon, and Theiner, his relationship with Alpers was more complex. Alpers was the star among the new assistant professors. Somewhat reminiscent of the actor Liam Neeson, he was tall, with an equine face, and a commanding presence. He was a skilled and popular teacher, and he always appeared to be in competition with his colleagues, especially with Stanley. It was as if he sensed that in a very short time Stanley would take the academic world by storm. Stanley wanted to be closer friends with Alpers but found it difficult because—whether deserved or not—he and others always had the sense that Alpers was judging them and finding them lacking. It may have been an accurate assessment of Alpers, or it may have been some projection or sense of inadequacy on their part, but the fact is that Alpers remained somewhat detached from several of his colleagues. Stanley and Alpers developed a sense of mutual respect tempered by a professional reserve toward each other. Nonetheless, Stanley held him in high esteem throughout the decades and considered his book on Edmund Spenser's *Fairie Queene* to be one of the finest works of scholarship of its kind. He would comment privately, "I never saw Alpers do anything that wasn't exemplary." Decades later at a reception they would reminisce fondly about their days together at Berkeley.

Most of the young Berkeley faculty who had come from the Harvard graduate program in English had at one time or another served as teaching assistants helping the distinguished Reuben A. Brower teach his famous undergraduate course, HUM 6, The Interpretation of Literature—a rigorous course in close reading. The Harvard group—including Alpers, Booth, Don Friedman, and Stephen Orgel—would on occasion reminisce nostalgically about their experience helping the eminent professor teach this legendary course. This shared experience helped make these junior professors an especially close and cohesive group. That experience also had a significant influence on the type of scholarship these professors undertook. They all had a deep intellectual commitment to close, analytical reading.

There was a good deal of cohesion among the junior faculty in the 1960s and 1970s for a variety of reasons. One is that many faculty tended to live near the campus. Also, the department held many functions where faculty got together both to socialize and to listen to talks and engage in evening discussions. In those days, the graduate program was especially labor intensive: almost everyone assisted in master's oral examinations since all the key literary areas were represented, so all the junior faculty became especially knowledgeable about their colleagues' areas and research interests. This helped to solidify their sense of belonging to a group. These young scholars, including Stanley, were all engaging in a similar type of scholarship that embraced but went beyond close reading to address reader expectations and rhetorical structures. They would invite one another to their classrooms to give guest presentations, and there was a significant amount of cross-pollination at the time. It was an intellectually fertile and exciting period. The young Berkeley crowd would produce several major works before the decade's end, including Alpers's *The Poetry of "The Faerie Queene"* (1967), Booth's *An Essay on Shakespeare's Sonnets* (1969), and Stanley's groundbreaking *Surprised by Sin* (1967).

In those days, some of the senior faculty in the department were skeptical about criticism that paid attention to issues of religion. The assumption was that if you were interested in these concerns, you were part of a "God Squad" interested in proselytizing, or that you would argue that the very presence of Christian references in a poem made that poem work better. Despite this skepticism, scholars such as Stanley and George Starr did not shy away from pointing out, when relevant, that religion or religious views played an important role in a given work. They were not interested in proselytizing (certainly, Stanley had no interest in furthering the agenda of Christianity), but they were interested in showing all formative influences on a work. Especially in the case of such poets as Herbert and Milton, a knowledge of their religious views and the religious context of their works was essential to a full understanding of those works. After hearing a number of Stanley's talks, most of these skeptical senior faculty became convinced that Stanley was not part of some God Squad but was, in fact, making valuable contributions to our understanding of literature.

In his first year at Berkeley, Stanley attended a series of courses on the German philosopher Martin Heidegger given by Hubert Dreyfus. Stanley had met Dreyfus through John R. Searle, an Oxford-trained philosopher of mind and language and a colleague with Dreyfus in the Berkeley philosophy department. Dreyfus was an exceedingly energetic, lively, and smart scholar, which immediately attracted Stanley to him. This preparation in Heidegger's thought would soon come in useful as his own work became more philosophical, and his friendship with both Dreyfus and especially Searle would be enduring.

Stanley's career took an abrupt and unexpected turn in 1963. He had begun his career as a medievalist, and he had been making many plans to further that career. He had begun discussions with a Skelton scholar at UCLA, Robert Kinsman, to coedit a new edition of the works of Skelton with him. He had also made tentative plans with his colleague Alain Renoir, who was an Anglo-Saxon specialist and son of Jean Renoir the filmmaker (and grandson of the French Impressionist painter), to teach Renoir's classes when he went on leave. And he had taught and would teach the medieval period for several years, especially the four-teenth century, mostly the works of Chaucer. Then in 1963, Berkeley's prominent Miltonist, C. A. Patrides, was awarded a research grant just before the semester was to begin, so he would not be teaching his Milton course. The department chair summoned Stanley to his office and said to his surprise, "Stanley, I want you to teach Patrides's Milton course. Are you up to it?" Stanley thought it unwise to reveal that he had never even taken a Milton course as a student, so he replied without hesitation, "Sure, I'd be happy to." The chair was relieved because the Milton course was a popular and important course in the curriculum.

Having agreed to teach a course on a subject he knew little about, Stanley really had to scramble. Yes, he had read *Paradise Lost* five times during his catch-up reading marathon that first summer at Yale, but Milton was a huge hole in his reading. He knew that he would need to engage in intensive studying to do a credible job in this class. He met the class on the first day of the semester and assigned an independent research project that would take up the first three weeks of the semester; this bought him the time to immerse himself in Milton's works as well as the critical literature. He read everything Miltonic, day and night for three weeks—the poetry, the prose, the critical literature. By the end of this immersion, he was hooked. He had not expected to become so enthralled by Milton, but he realized with great clarity that he had fi-nally found his real niche—and, luckily, Milton was a major figure. He sat back in his chair, and the words of Talbot Donaldson echoed in his head: "Okay, do your dissertation on Skelton, but if you're going to get anywhere in the profession, you are going to have to write scholarship on a major figure, as well."

He likened his experience of becoming unexpectedly hooked to a similar dynamic that undergraduates commonly experience: they enroll in a literature course on an unfamiliar author or literary era assuming that they are going to have a disagreeable experience, that they will not be able to connect in any meaningful way to the material, but then they unexpectedly find the material to be challenging and engaging, and, before long, they cannot get enough of it. Stanley was especially taken with the verbal effects that Milton achieved at the sentence level. He would marvel at particularly masterful sentences. He would read a passage and sit back, thinking, "How could anybody have done that? It's just amazing. Linguistic acrobatics, a tour de force." Indeed, his admiration for well-wrought sentences, spurred by Milton's linguistic dexterity, would inspire a lifelong attention to "perfect" sentences, culminating in his book *How to Write a Sentence: And How to Read One* (2011).

Stanley would continue to teach a course in fifteenth-century literature, primarily because the work was so unusual and rarely read anymore. He would say to his students on the first day of class, "After completing this class you will be able to impress anyone at a literary cocktail party because nobody will have read this material except you!" Despite his commitment to that work, his fascination with Milton would continue to grow and almost become all consuming. One course in particular would solidify his transition to becoming a dedicated Miltonist. During the 1960s, the Berkeley English department sponsored a special summer program in which they would select ten high-achieving undergraduates who they believed would be good candidates for graduate school, and they paid for them to attend a special graduate seminar on a literary figure or work. Students from any university could apply for the program, and admission was highly competitive, so the ten students who were chosen in any given year were especially gifted. During the summer of 1964, Stanley taught the course on *Paradise Lost* to ten Berkeley students, including Bob Avakian, the legendary political activist who one day would become the chairman of the Revolutionary Communist Party, USA. It was an extraordinary seminar, very intense—so intense, in fact, that three marriages came out of that summer's course, a testimony to the erotic component of both Stanley's intense teaching and of *Paradise Lost*. This experience clinched it. There was no turning back.

He has always had a genuine passion for teaching. Although many research universities then (as they do now) discouraged faculty from teaching in the summer so that they would have the summer to conduct their research, Stanley always taught summer school when he could. While at Berkeley he would be paid $500 per summer course, which would have been almost 10 percent of his annual salary at the time. He enjoyed—and needed—the extra salary, but it was his passion for teaching that drove him to accept practically every offer to teach. On a few occasions he turned down course reductions simply because he wanted to be in front of a class. During the 1970s and 1980s he would usually teach during the summers in the School of Criticism and Theory, and even when he became dean of a large and complex college years later, he continued to teach—a workload many deans could not imagine undertaking. Years later when he would have a summer house in upstate New York, he would interrupt his vacationing to travel two hours to Cornell to teach a one-week seminar. The fact that he has been so dedicated throughout his career to teaching—even to teaching first-year composition (he chose to teach composition as dean)—refutes a common criticism of Stanley: that he is an Ivy League academic out of touch with students. As he once said, "If you're an actor, where do you most want to be? You want to be on stage in front of your audience. The same is true if you're a teacher: you want to be in the classroom."

Stanley became notorious for using a tape recorder in his classes. He realized early on that sometimes in the give-and-take of class discussions he would work out an explanation of a topic in an especially elegant or cogent way. Before using the tape recorder, he would often struggle after the class session to reconstruct his exact phrasing. Once he began using the recorder, however, he was able to capture his improvised explanations. At first, he would transcribe the tapes himself; later he would have a modest research stipend that allowed him to pay students to transcribe them. He would not tape the entire class, only the parts when he was speaking. Occasionally, if the conversation got particularly intense and insightful, he would let the recorder capture the entire discussion. The gems that he would extract from these tapes would later show up in his published writings.

During the summer of 1965, Stanley would make an acquaintance that would turn into a lifetime friendship. The British novelist and literary critic David Lodge was spending the summer in San Francisco with his wife Mary and their two young children after having spent a year in the States as a Harkness Commonwealth Fellow. Lodge was not affiliated with a university that summer, but he made contact with Berkeley's English department through a British colleague who was a visiting professor there that year. He and his wife invited the Lodges to dinner with Stanley and Adrienne, and they all bonded instantly. Shortly thereafter the Fishes invited the Lodges to dinner in their house, with its stunning view of San Francisco Bay. Stanley then took Lodge to his first baseball game, at Candlestick Park, and they soon became good friends. Lodge would go on to pen a series of popular novels satirizing campus life, some of which included the character Morris Zapp, whom he fashioned in large part after Stanley. Lodge considered Stanley one of his oldest friends in American academe. In 2001 they would reunite on stage at the Chicago Humanities Festival to discuss Lodge's novel *Thinks . . .*

That same year, 1965, Yale University Press published Stanley's first book, *John Skelton's Poetry*, a revision of his dissertation. Beginning at the end of the nineteenth century and lasting into the 1970s, when it was refashioned, Yale University Press sponsored a book series called Yale Studies in English. Although the series would publish books by Yale faculty, it was largely an outlet for Yale graduates to publish revisions of their dissertations—a common practice among university presses in the twentieth century until economic forces beginning in the early 1970s forced the presses to become more competitive and less dependent on substantial subsidies from their institutions. Among the many notable books published in the Yale series are Harry Berger's *The Allegorical Temper*, Harold Bloom's *Shelley's Mythmaking*, Stephen Greenblatt's *Sir Walter Raleigh*, and George Ridenour's *The Style of Don Juan*.

Stanley did not know it at the time, but his future second wife, the literary critic Jane Tompkins, had been invited to publish her dissertation in the series but declined. She was a graduate student in the Yale program in English but a few years behind Stanley. They did not know one another at the time, although Jane remembers Stanley visiting a class she was taking from renowned literary scholar Thomas Greene. After she finished her dissertation on Melville's prose style and had received the offer to include it in the series, she asked the advice of a trusted faculty mentor. "Why don't you wait a year or two and spend some time revising it," she advised. Jane had not yet developed a strong sense of self-confidence about her intellectual work, so she dutifully acquiesced. Decades later, in recalling this "extraordinarily bad piece of advice" from the faculty advisor, Stanley would comment, "Even telling this story gets me ill."

John Skelton's Poetry was a break with standard New Critical values and practices. The New Criticism was committed to a slavish preoccupation with the text and a refusal to consider extratextual factors such a historical context, the author's biography, and certainly the author's intentions in a poem. Fish decried "the almost conspiratorial unwillingness" of critics to acknowledge that Skelton is "in any way involved in his own poetry," and he worked from the original (and to some shocking) premise that the most productive reading of a Skelton poem was to understand it first as a reflection of the narrator's (not necessarily the poet's) internal state of mind and to move from an analysis of the speaker's psychology to external considerations, such as scene and context. His readings of Skelton's poetry were, consequently, thoroughly rhetorical and, as such, were a substantial departure from typical New Critical practice as propounded by his mentors, Cleanth Brooks and William Wimsatt. While this book did not receive the kind of critical attention that his next book, *Surprised by Sin*, would, it was just as revolutionary in its own right, self-consciously breaking with the New Critical tradition and offering a reading that was unapologetically rhetorical and that foreshadowed the more full-blown "Reader Response" reading in *Surprised by Sin*. Years later, his major professor, Talbot Donaldson, would say to colleagues in private that this was the best work of criticism on Skelton's poetry that he had ever read—high praise from a demanding perfectionist. Adrienne beamed when she first opened their advance copy of the book and read its dedication: "To Adrienne," followed by two lines from Skelton: "For I have gravyd her within the secret wall / Of my trew hart, to love her best of all."

During the fall of 1966, the seven professors who joined the Berkeley English department in 1962 underwent midprobationary performance evaluations. Stanley's and George Starr's records were so stellar that they were accelerated to tenure and promotion to associate professors, effective the next fall semester. They were the only ones in their cohort of seven to be accelerated to tenure. Indeed, Alkon and Theiner would eventually carve out successful careers in other institutions. Alkon would go on to become a chaired professor of American literature at the University of Southern California, the president of the American Society for Eighteenth-Century Studies, and a scholar of science fiction literature.

With tenure under his belt, Stanley redirected his main attention away from his department and Berkeley itself and toward the national scene. He began to take on a number of visiting appointments and countless speaking engagements. That year, he received a grant from the American Council of Learned Societies to spend a half year researching at the British Museum, so Adrienne and Stanley traveled abroad with their newly adopted daughter, Susan. On a whim, they decided they would embark on a whirlwind tour of Western Europe. A lifelong automobile enthusiast, Stanley purchased a sleek Alfa Romeo. Universally accepted credit cards were still a novelty in 1966, so the couple bought a letter of credit from Barclays Bank that allowed them to obtain cash when needed from American Express offices. As they drove from town to town, they would periodically visit an American Express office to collect cash and mail from the States.

They picked up the Alfa Romeo in Milan, and then meandered first through the Italian Riviera and then through the French Riviera. When they arrived in Spain, they stayed in Costa del Sol for a few days, and later in Seville. To the dismay of the local police, drag racing was quite common on the streets of Seville, and it is not surprising that the enfant terrible found himself in a number of harrowing races, careening recklessly through the quiet Seville streets. They then returned to France, first to the luxurious seaside town of Biarritz on the Bay of Biscay, and then to the rich wine and food country, before arriving in Paris to catch their breath and soak in the luscious Parisian cuisine. They then briefly visited Denmark before finally settling down in England, first living in Chelsea before they found a cute little bungalow with a spiral staircase on a side street around the corner from Abbey Road Studios, made famous by the Beatles. Stanley would spend the next six months in the British Museum writing *Surprised by Sin*—in longhand.

During their romp through the Riviera, they stopped in an American Express office to collect mail from the States, and there was a letter awaiting them from the chair of the English department at Washington University in St. Louis, Missouri, asking if he would come as a visiting professor for a semester to teach Milton. St. Louis did not seem particularly appealing to him, and he could see Adrienne already looking askance at him, but it was an honor to be asked to be a visiting professor. Such positions afforded him and his work increased exposure. Besides, he needed the money. His salary then was only $5,500, so any additional funds would be greatly appreciated. He proposed to Adrienne that he make them a preposterous offer—twice his Berkeley salary—and if they said no, then there would be no loss; if they said yes, well, all the better. She agreed, and he fired off a letter to the chair. When they arrived at the next town in their tour and collected their mail from the American Express office, he was astonished to find a letter from the chair of the English department at Washington University eagerly accepting Stanley's preposterous offer. My God, what do I do now? he thought to himself. After some reflection, he wrote back, saying, "I'm not sure that this will work because I will already have been gone from Berkeley for a year, and I'm not sure that they would then allow me to be away for still another half a year." The chair wrote back, saying, "Oh, we have already cleared that with your department chair at Berkeley. You are free to join us." Suddenly, he felt trapped. He could see that Adrienne was not thrilled about living in St. Louis. At least it wasn't Madison, Wisconsin, or Urbana, Illinois. A semester in St. Louis couldn't be that bad.

They returned to the States with a month to spare before he was to report for duty at Washington University, so they decided to stay in New York City. They rented a place for a month across the street from the Dakota on Seventy-second Street, the famous residence at one time or another of Lauren Bacall, Leonard Bernstein, Judy Garland, Boris Karloff, Rudolf Nureyev, Rex Reed, and John Lennon—and where Lennon would be gunned down by Mark David Chapman in December of 1980. They reveled in the delights of the Big Apple before reluctantly setting out for their new adventure in St. Louis. They both were jazz aficionados, so they made sure to take in as many performances as they could while there.

Their time at Washington University would not be especially pleasant. They found great difficulty in renting an acceptable apartment, so they were forced to stay in an overpriced hotel until they could secure appropriate accommodations. Eventually Stanley was able to find a smart garden apartment in a small, affluent suburb called Webster Groves.

When he first accepted the offer to come to Washington University as a visiting professor, he had not been aware that the department had arranged his visit as a "look-see visit," a common practice in which a department would invite a high-level or promising scholar to campus for a semester to determine if that person was such a good fit for the department that they should tender an offer of a permanent position. The department's Miltonist, Joseph Summers, had recently taken a position at the University of Rochester, and he had given them nine recommendations of up-and-coming stars in Milton studies; the department was hoping to attract Stanley—if he proved to be a good fit—to join their faculty.

Before arriving in St. Louis, he had discovered that there would be a gap of a month and a half between his final stipend check from the American Council of Learned Societies and his first paycheck from Washington University, so he had made an arrangement whereby he would receive proportionately more salary early in the semester and less later in the semester. On his first day he strode into the English department office and exchanged pleasantries with the chair, Jarvis Thurston, who was married to Mona Van Duyn, the accomplished poet who would go on to win the Pulitzer Prize and become the first woman named poet laureate of the United States. Thurston mentioned casually, "By the way, the arrangement that you made about having your salary front-loaded won't work because we have a new computer system and it can't handle that kind of thing." Shocked, Stanley explained his situation and asked, "Well, what do you advise?" Unsympathetic, the chair replied, "Well, I can introduce you to the bank that my wife and I do business with. I'm sure they could give you a loan at a decent rate." Stanley looked at him in disbelief. "May I use your phone?" he asked. He dialed the university operator and asked to be connected to the vice president for finance and administration. The department chair stared at him in horror—the vice president was many levels above him in the institutional hierarchy. To everyone's astonishment, the vice president accepted the call. Stanley calmly explained his situation and pointed out that he had come to the university under a certain arrangement and now the university was reneging and advising him to secure a loan. Thurston first turned white and then various shades of red. Stanley said to the vice president, "Here's the deal: either by the end of the day the situation has been resolved so that the agreement that I thought we had is once again in place, or I'm leaving immediately for Berkeley." Within an hour, the original arrangement was reinstated. The department chair was humiliated; it had been his job to rectify this problem and not let it rise to the vice presidential level, but he had failed.

Clearly, Stanley did not start out on the right foot with the department chair, but he was not about to be taken advantage of. A second incident that ensured that the department would not make him an offer occurred shortly thereafter. The department's medievalist was very friendly to Stanley in the first few weeks and liked to chat with him about his work on Skelton and Chaucer. Then, one day he approached Stanley and said, "By the way, we have a little anti–Vietnam War group that meets every Wednesday evening, and we would be pleased if you would join us." Stanley looked at him intently for a moment and replied, "I'm afraid I'm on the other side of that question." The medievalist recoiled and blurted out, "There *is* no other side." He had mistakenly assumed that because Stanley was a professor at Berkeley—a hotbed of radicalism—he would naturally hold the same liberal political views that he did. He never spoke to Stanley again.

Stanley was making friends with several faculty, but he could tell that his candidacy at Washington University was dead in the water. He never wanted a position at the institution, but so long as people believed he was a potential candidate, uncomfortable institutional politics were in play. Adrienne came to the rescue. "Why don't you simply announce that you are formally withdrawing from consideration for the Milton position," she said. "That will take the pressure off of everybody." He immediately saw the wisdom of this, and picked up the phone and informed the department chair. This was the right thing to do; the rest of the semester was much less tense since no one felt obligated to take sides for or against the emerging superstar.

Adrienne and Stanley finally made their way back to Berkeley, and awaiting them was an advance copy of Stanley's masterpiece, *Surprised by Sin: The Reader in "Paradise Lost."* It was soon to be a critical sensation. It accomplished two major goals: it transformed Milton scholarship, and it forever changed the craft of literary criticism. Before this groundbreaking book was published, Milton critics typically found themselves in one of two theoretical camps: those who read *Paradise Lost* as glorifying God as the hero of the work, and those who read it as identifying with the strength and audacity of Satan—that is, with Satan as the prototypical heroic, revolutionary figure. Clearly, these are two seemingly irreconcilable interpretations, and Milton scholars battled over this ground for decades. *Surprised by Sin* successfully reconciled these positions by shifting the site of interpretation from the words on the page to the effect the words have on the reader. Briefly, the poem causes readers first to identify with Satan—that is, to fall from grace, to sin—and then to be saved, to acknowledge their fallen nature and to reembrace God. In other words, the poet intentionally and skillfully created the tension between readers' affinity first to Satan and then to God in order to create a psychological (and pedagogical) effect in readers: they are surprised to find themselves in a state of sin and immediately attempt to save themselves.

This kind of reading was unprecedented, and it was heretical to the New Criticism, which was in the ascendency during the 1960s, although it was increasingly coming under attack. The New Critics held that the role of the literary critic was to treat the text as an object placed under their critical lens. Meaning resided in the text, and extratextual concerns such as historical or cultural information or the author's intention should not be the concern of the literary scholar. The professional critic was to focus narrowly but deeply on close analysis of the text. *Surprised by Sin* shifted the critical focus from meaning as embedded in the text to meaning as produced by the reader in the act of reading—a revolutionary challenge to the New Criticism and one of the first of a flood of challenges to critical orthodoxy that would soon be dubbed Reader Response Criticism. While Stanley was certainly not the only leader of this novel critical approach, he soon would become one of its main intellectual champions, and he did more to articulate its theoretical principles than any of his contemporaries.

One misty spring day in 1969, Stanley was strolling down the hallway that passed by Berkeley's English department office, and he noticed a flyer on a bulletin board announcing that a professor in Paris would be spending the summer at Berkeley and was seeking to trade his apartment in Paris for a house or apartment in Berkeley for the summer months. Stanley was intrigued. After all, this was the dawn of a revolution in critical thought led primarily by French intellectuals, most of them residing in Paris. The French theorists were taking the intellectual world by storm, and Stanley was not yet fully familiar with the emerging poststructuralist discourses. That evening over dinner he told Adrienne about the flyer and asked tentatively, "What do you think?" The consummate cosmopolitan, she didn't hesitate. "Absolutely! Let's do it." He immediately made arrangements. This summer in Paris would be a major turning point in his intellectual development.

This was an especially momentous time politically. The previous year, 1968, was the year of the Tet Offensive and the My Lai massacre in Vietnam, increased and sometimes violent antiwar protests, the assassination of Robert Kennedy and Martin Luther King Jr., the riot outside the Democratic National Convention in Chicago, and widespread unrest on college campuses, including Berkeley. In France, workers and students united in mass protests against the state, nearly toppling the government in May of 1968. In 1969 hundreds of thousands of antiwar protestors took to the streets in the United States; students seized Harvard University's administration building; and the Stonewall Riots in New York City marked the beginning of gay rights activism in the United States. It was the year of the Manson Family killings and the Chappaquiddick incident.

This was also an intellectually heady time in Paris and in literary theory in general, a time of intellectual ferment and rebellion. An historic conference held at Johns Hopkins University in 1966 had sparked intense interest in poststructuralism among intellectuals in the United States. Attending were Roland Barthes, Jacques Derrida, and Jacques Lacan, among others. At the conference Derrida presented his now famous attack on structuralism "Structure, Sign, and Play in the Human Sciences." A year later Barthes published his *Elements of Semiology* and "The Death of the Author." By 1969 the intellectual world was abuzz with revolution—a violent break with the intellectual past. The intelligentsia—especially young academics—all seemed to be reading not only Barthes and Derrida, but Jean Baudrillard, Hélène Cixous, Michel Foucault, Julia Kristeva, Luce Irigaray, and Jean-François Lyotard. Stanley's timing could not have been better.

Adrienne and Stanley were met at Paris's Orly airport by Seymour Chatman, a professor of rhetoric at Berkeley and one of the foremost scholars of narratology. Chatman, who had been an instructor of Stanley's at Penn, had become an insider in the Paris intellectual circuit and had an entrée into an ongoing seminar at Vincennes populated by people who were steeped in or to some extent were beginning to produce this new theoretical work. Stanley was invited to join them. One of the participants was Bruce Morrissette, who translated and wrote about the works of the French author and filmmaker Alain Robbe-Grillet. The literary theorist Tzvetan Todorov would make appearances at the seminar, as well. Poststructuralist theory was new to Stanley, and this immersion in it, particularly during this intellectually fertile time and in what some might consider the capital city of this French intellectual movement, left an indelible mark on him. He could not wait to teach a class in literary theory.

Besides learning the fundamentals of poststructuralist theory, Stanley learned another lesson that he would never forget. One day he arrived at the seminar, and the participants were milling around waiting for the session to begin. They were excitedly discussing a sensational court case currently in the French news: a group of people were being prosecuted for having robbed a train. Stanley listened to the animated discussion for a while, and he could sense that the seminar participants felt that the defendants should not be prosecuted. In all his Anglo-American, empiricist naiveté, he asked, "Do you mean that they didn't do it?" The group stared at him for a few seconds, and then one replied with disdain, "No, it was a *political* crime"—meaning that the perpetrators did it for the right reasons so it should not be classified as a crime. This was his first introduction to a way of thinking in which a simple question like "Did he or didn't he commit the crime?" was replaced by "What kind of act was it?" If it was a political act, then the naming of it as a crime was an act of what the group called "the hegemonic bourgeoisie." This was an ideology, a way of thinking he had never encountered before. It would have a profound effect on his understanding of how rhetoric works, and this concept would make its way into many if not most of his theoretical works over the next decades. He learned from this episode that people don't simply arrive at a position or belief because they have been persuaded by the logic or "reasonableness" of someone's argument; they arrive at a position or belief because it fits into their structure of beliefs. They then seek the available means of persuasion to justify that belief, both to themselves and to others. Evidence that bolsters their position is displayed; evidence that does not is dismissed.

Stanley struggled with the Bohemian mind-set he found in Paris. At the time, he was in his early thirties and several of the participants were in their twenties. Despite his reputation as a bad boy, he did have a strong sense of right and wrong. He always remembered the lessons of Rabbi Bohnen. In one session of the seminar he had expressed an interest in one of the books that had been mentioned in the discussion. The next day one of the participants presented him with a gift copy of the book. "This is very generous of you," Stanley replied to the baby-faced revolutionary. The young man grinned and said, presaging Abbie Hoffman's soon-to-be-published *Steal this Book*, "Don't worry about it. I stole it." Stanley was horrified: "I can't accept this book." Once again, he was exhibiting his outdated bourgeois mentality.

As soon as he returned to Berkeley, he arranged to teach a course in the various new and emerging literary theories, and he would continue to teach this course throughout the years. He organized the course in such a way as to ease students slowly into the more revolutionary theories, so as to minimize the shock. He began with what would not have seemed so odd at the time: statistical and computer stylistics of the type furthered by scholars such as Louis T. Milic. Stylistic analysis was a form of empirical analysis of text that allowed the researcher to make inferences and draw conclusions about a work based on linguistic patterns within the text. He then moved to the social semiotics of M. A. K. Halliday, which also entailed analysis of linguistic patterns. From there the class progressed to speech act theory, which was new at the time, but nonetheless not unfamiliar since it also involved charting certain kinds of linguistic patterns to determine meaning. John L. Austin's *How to Do Things with Words* had been published in 1962 and was by then well known, as was work by Richard Ohmann and Stanley's colleague John R. Searle, so speech act theory would seem fresh but not threatening. From this point, he would introduce the students to structuralist thought, focusing first on the work of Vladimir Propp, the Russian formalist scholar, especially his *Morphology of the Folktale*, and then on the work of Claude Lévi-Strauss, the French anthropologist and ethnologist. Having brought the class methodically to structuralism, he then made the leap to the new poststructuralist theories. They would read Barthes,

Derrida, Foucault, and many of the new intellectual works emerging at the time. He would also work in his own Reader Response Criticism that grew out of his work on *Surprised by Sin*, supplemented by the work of Michael Riffaterre, Wolfgang Iser, and Hans Robert Jauss.

In the fall of 1969, a recent Yale graduate, Stephen Greenblatt, joined the Berkeley faculty. Greenblatt would later become known as the father of the critical approach dubbed New Historicism, an approach that Stanley would criticize on a number of occasions as being too concerned with cultural politics and not enough with the literary text under examination. At a departmental cocktail reception early in the fall semester, Greenblatt was doing his best to meet his new colleagues when Stanley, cocktail in hand, strode boldly up to him and announced, perhaps a little too loudly, "So, *you're* the rookie of the year." Greenblatt was at once amused and horrified: he understood that Stanley was paying him a special compliment by singling him out of the dozen or so English faculty hired that year as *the* rookie of that year's crop, but he was embarrassed that others heard the exchange, perhaps even some of his peers. Like many of the young Berkeley faculty in the 1960s, Stanley wore a pair of striped bell-bottom trousers and a sports jacket. The two began to talk and soon developed a mutual admiration for one another.

Some weeks later, Stanley received news that he had been awarded a Guggenheim Fellowship to work on what would become *Self-Consuming Artifacts*. He would spend the summer that year as a visiting professor at Sir George Williams University in Montreal teaching Milton and literary criticism and working on his book.

Stanley was making substantial progress on his book when, in 1971, Johns Hopkins University invited him to come to Hopkins for a semester as a visiting professor—another look-see appointment. Stanley had become close friends through Milton Society of America meetings with two Renaissance studies scholars: Jackson Cope from Hopkins and Edward W. Tayler from Columbia. He described the trio as "short, feisty, and kind of outsized personalities at times." Jack had successfully campaigned to bring Stanley to Hopkins, and so Adrienne, Stanley, Susan, and their Dachshund, Abdiel, traveled to a new adventure in Baltimore. They rented a cute little row house in Rodgers Forge, a historic community just north of the city line. They would all come to love Baltimore, and Stanley would soon discover the substantial difference between a good public university like Berkeley and a well-endowed, elite, private institution like Johns Hopkins.

Hopkins seemed devoted to the well-being and comfort of its faculty. The faculty in the English department all enjoyed two-day-a-week teaching schedules and were guaranteed a semester off after every five semesters of teaching. Because Hopkins was a highly competitive elite institution, the faculty were not overwhelmed with great numbers of students; the classes were small, and the students were exceptionally well prepared. The department was small as well, perhaps ten or twelve faculty. Stanley was drawn immediately to the intense intellectual atmosphere of Hopkins. While faculty were expected to excel in all areas, to be superior teachers and leading scholars in their disciplines, especially important at Hopkins was a professor's performance in lectures given under the auspices of the Tudor and Stuart Club, a longtime Hopkins tradition.

Fashioned roughly after Yale's Elizabethan Club, the Tudor and Stuart Club is an endowed literary club dedicated to fostering the study of English literature in the Tudor and Stuart periods. It was endowed in 1918 by Sir William Osler, one of the original faculty at the Johns Hopkins Medical School. The club amassed an impressive library, published the prestigious learned journal *ELH* (*English Literary History*), and sponsored public lectures on literary topics. The club had a dedicated room in Gilman Hall, where its monthly lectures were held. It was a somewhat uncomfortable room with uncomfortable chairs, and it was invariably packed full of spectators for each lecture. While anyone could attend, most audience members were associated with the English department— faculty, graduate students, even undergraduates.

The much-anticipated part of each event was the long question-and-answer period. These exchanges were grueling and exhilarating intellectual battles. Some participants thought of them as akin to a fraternity hazing, some as an academic contact sport. As Stanley described it, "You could win your spurs or lose them in the Tudor and Stuart room, but no act that you performed in the context of the academy went unnoticed there." It was during these sessions that your mettle was on display. The sessions were governed by unwritten rituals—who asked the first questions and in what order. While for many lecturers the Tudor and Stuart Club sessions were an unbearable pressure cooker, and many left embarrassed or vanquished, these sessions seemed to be tailor-made for Stanley. He loved the verbal dueling, the thrust and parry, the intellectual intensity. He had discovered an academic version of his beloved basketball.

Of course, those who did not understand the rarified rituals of the Tudor and Stuart Club could quickly run into trouble. You were expected to be appropriately agonistic, but never inappropriately so. This happened to the famous classicist William Arrowsmith, who came to Hopkins for a short time but did not survive. Apparently, he thought that it was his job to knock the esteemed Hugh Kenner off his pedestal. A student of Marshall McLuhan, Kenner was a Yale PhD and a specialist in modernist literature, especially James Joyce and Ezra Pound. He was one of Hopkins's most distinguished scholars, and his masterpiece, *The Pound Era*, had just come out in 1971. He was an imposing figure. Arrowsmith was a direct contemporary of Kenner with an equivalent if not more impressive academic pedigree, having studied at Princeton and Oxford. To his detriment, Arrowsmith underestimated Kenner's mettle, and his savage attack on him at a Tudor and Stuart Club session backfired. He left Hopkins soon thereafter.

One day Stanley and two Hopkins faculty members, Jack Cope and Don Howard, decided to throw an especially large party, which they dubbed the First Annual Baltimore Bash (there would only be one). They held the event in the building where both Cope and Howard lived: Highfield House, an impressive high-rise condominium designed by Ludwig Mies van der Rohe, the father of modern architecture. The party was quite a success. The next day they met to divide the leftover liquor, and when Stanley and Adrienne then went to retrieve their car, they discovered his beloved Porsche impossibly pinned in by a car parked immediately behind it. It took Stanley a full fifteen minutes to extricate his Porsche without scratching it. He was furious at the driver for his inconsiderate behavior, so the enfant terrible decided to punish him. He picked up a good-size rock from a nearby garden and smashed it forcefully into the headlight of the offending car. There was only one problem: he neglected to let go of the rock, and a flying shard of glass slashed his wrist, cutting the artery. Blood was gushing everywhere. Adrienne was livid. How could he be so childish? The tough boy from the streets of Providence had emerged and struck out at injustice, but he had paid for his transgression. As Adrienne stanched the bleeding with a scarf, he thought of Rabbi Bohnen and his strict sense of right and wrong.

Although Stanley felt especially at home at Hopkins, he would soon receive some disappointing news. One day about two-thirds of the way through the semester, he was on his way to attend a talk by a Milton scholar from the University of Washington, Arnold Stein. The Hopkins English department had invited him to give a talk on his recent research. His most recent book, *On Milton's Poetry*, an edited collection of recent Milton scholarship, had come out in 1970. Stanley knew and respected Stein's work and was eager to hear his lecture. As he climbed the stairs from the building's basement entrance to the floor where the English department offices were located, he spied Stein being led ceremoniously down the hall by the department chair, Ronald Paulson—the very Paulson who had graduated from Yale, taken, and then vacated a position at the University of Illinois, and whose slot at Illinois the Yale power brokers had attempted to fill with the newly graduated Stanley Fish. Stanley was stunned; he immediately recognized the unmistakable posture of the two. My god, he thought to himself. This is a recruitment visit. Stein was in direct competition with Stanley for the Hopkins position. Stein was already a well-established, distinguished scholar with a very respectable record; he would be the ideal candidate for the Hopkins position. Stanley had a sinking feeling in his stomach. He was tired of Berkeley, he had grown to love Hopkins, and he was ready for a move. Stein complicated matters because in many ways he was the logical choice. And, in fact, that was what happened: Hopkins hired Stein soon thereafter. Never one to hold a grudge, Stanley would later, in 1982, guest-edit a special issue of *ELH* in honor of Stein.

Disappointed, Stanley, Adrienne, Susan and the dog then made the long, monotonous trip back to the West Coast.

That next year, 1972, Jackson Cope, the Renaissance studies scholar, left Hopkins for a position at the University of Southern California (USC). When he arrived, he convinced the English department to invite Stanley to come to USC for the 1973–74 academic year as an endowed professor: the Leo S. Bing Professor of English. Stanley packed up his family again and rented a house in the San Fernando Valley, just below Mulholland Road—a classic California-style ranch house complete with an in-ground swimming pool. Stanley's reputation as a major scholar had become well established by 1973. The two most sought-after Renaissance scholars during that period were Stanley and Angus Fletcher, the author of *The Prophetic Moment: An Essay on Spenser* (1971) among other noted works. Universities courted them, journals invited them to serve on their editorial boards, and university presses sought their endorsement of soon-to-be-published books. Suddenly, Stanley was flooded with offers. In that year alone, he received offers from eight institutions, including Columbia, the University of Connecticut, the University of Virginia, and Hopkins. He was delighted to receive the Hopkins offer. Late in 1972 he had received a cryptic note from the distinguished Hopkins romanticist Earl Wasserman inquiring if he would be interested in a permanent position at Hopkins. If so, said Wasserman, he would test the waters and might be able to exert "some small influence" on his colleagues. Wasserman, of course, had substantial influence, and a generous offer soon arrived.

Stanley and Adrienne's year at USC had not been especially pleasant. During that year Stanley experienced two relatively brief bouts of depression—a rare occurrence for him. He was overwhelmed by lethargy and inertia. He had no energy and lost interest in all of the pursuits that normally made him happy. The second of these bouts had been persisting for several weeks when he realized that he had to take decisive action to end it. Driving had always grounded him, so, instinctually, he got into his car and made the six-hundred-mile trip back to his home in Berkeley. He had some business to tend to concerning their house, and he felt that the long drive might be therapeutic, affording him an extended period of time to reflect and relax. He was right. During the course of the trip, the depression lifted just as mysteriously as it had taken hold of him. Perhaps contributing to his ennui was the fact that he had become quite disillusioned with Berkeley. He felt that it was simply not becoming the first-rate English department that he believed it had once promised to become. He felt that even with its collection of stellar faculty it had become complacent and too institutionally comfortable with its status.

The last straw for Stanley was a departmental meeting in the 1972–73 academic year devoted to a debate over whether to voluntarily increase the course load of senior professors from two-two to three-two. Stanley had been promoted to professor in 1971, so this increase would materially affect him. Those proposing the change gave three reasons. First, it was argued that by willingly voting for a load increase, the faculty would then be in a better position to defend themselves when the administration asked them for more teaching, which was likely at the time. Stanley argued strenuously that whatever position the faculty are in when that request comes will be the baseline position, and they would be asked to further augment their teaching schedule from that point forward. The second reason given was that while senior professors were teaching two-two, their junior colleagues, who were worthy people, were teaching three-two. "Well that's easy," Stanley offered, "Give them two-two as well!" The third reason was so vague, metaphorical, and smacked of the kind of hippy communalism that Stanley so despised that he simply snorted in response to it: The voluntary increase will enrich our course offerings while putting us all on an equal footing. The debate lasted an excruciatingly long hour, and at a certain point Stanley leaned back in his chair and thought to himself: What am I doing in a place like this? People who think this way are hopeless!

While the debate raged, Stanley tuned out and lapsed into a meditative reverie. Yes, he used to enjoy borrowing books from his aunt and uncle in the flat downstairs in his childhood house, and yes he had been a good student—exceedingly good—and yes he had risen to the top of his academic discipline, and yes he would eventually be called America's chief public intellectual (a term he repudiated), but haunting him throughout the years was a deep and profound sense that in at least some ways the boy from the working-class streets of Providence really did not belong in academe. In certain ways, this was not his world. He compared himself to those (like his future wife, Jane Tompkins) who had been raised in a rich atmosphere of books, intellectual debates, art exhibits, symphonic concerts, and polite society. That was their world, not his. He thought back to his first semester at Berkeley, the incessant whispering about the red rug adorning his office, and about his well-appointed apartment and sleek car. He recalled that for the long Thanksgiving holiday that year, most of his colleagues traveled to the California countryside and camped out in tents by open fires. Adrienne and Stanley were not about to sleep on the ground. Comfort was too important. They traveled instead to southern California and stayed at an exclusive vacation resort in Palm Springs. His colleagues had been scandalized. A luxury resort? False values! He thought, too, of the prevailing academic psychology: how professors were expected—or, more to the point, willingly chose—to be self-sacrificing on a daily basis, to accept meager salaries, to take on an enormous amount of uncompensated labor (extra courses, dissertation and thesis advising, extra committee work), to accept abuse from their institutions and the public at large, to live a life of perpetual want. Let's face it, he thought to himself, academics are masochists; they love self-abnegation and self-abasement. Years later he would discuss this tendency of academics not only to tolerate mistreatment but to embrace it, to see it as a sign of their own virtue, in a controversial article entitled "The Unbearable Ugliness of Volvos."

Stanley and Adrienne were clearly ready to leave Berkeley, and they now had an embarrassment of riches in offers from very respectable universities. The decision was almost overwhelming. Each institution had made an attractive offer, and there were very good reasons to accept any one of them. To assist them in the decision, they constructed charts listing the various factors in the decision and assigning numerical values to each: quality of the university's library, department colleagues, salary, climate, school system, cultural life, and so on. Despite their Ben Franklin–style charts, they agonized over the decision. They eventually narrowed their choice to two: Hopkins and the University of Virginia. They went back and forth torturously between the two. Virginia seemed very attractive, and Stanley had friends on the faculty there, yet they both loved Hopkins and Baltimore. Finally, they chose Hopkins, but as soon as he plunked down the telephone receiver after having accepted the Hopkins appointment, he was haunted by reservations and misgivings. Did we make the right choice? The University of Virginia was the ultimate genteel institution, and they had made such an attractive offer. There were so many reasons to have accepted it. After a week or two, they both decided they had indeed made the right decision.

Chapter 4

Academic Utopia:
The Hopkins Years

As it turned out, Stanley's happiest years would be at Johns Hopkins. Despite his rise to international prominence and his appointments at a number of institutions after leaving Hopkins, he would never be able to duplicate its congenial and intellectually fertile atmosphere. Berkeley was a fine institution, and it was assembling a superb faculty, but Berkeley was nowhere near as intense an experience as Hopkins would be. Of all the institutions that he had been a part of throughout his entire career, the two that influenced him the most were Classical High and Johns Hopkins. He simply loved Hopkins, and after he left in 1986 for Duke, there would be many quiet moments when he secretly rued ever leaving his academic utopia. He loved the small size of the Hopkins department, the intellectual intensity, the Tudor and Stuart Club, the perks afforded to faculty members. It was a stellar faculty: Leo Braudy, Sharon Cameron, Frances Ferguson, Avrom Fleischman, Laurence Holland, Donald Howard, Hugh Kenner, Jerome McGann, Walter Benn Michaels, Stephen Orgel, Ronald Paulson, Arnold Stein, Barry Weller—each person in the department had a claim to being one of the top scholars in his field. Many were stars, if not superstars. Stanley would fall in love with this department.

Adrienne, Susan, and Stanley arrived back in Baltimore in the summer of 1974. Adrienne had previously traveled to Baltimore, studied the available houses on the market, and bought a magnificent Georgian-style house in the historic Mount Washington section of the city. Stanley did not see the house until they moved in; he had been preoccupied with settling affairs in California. Rumor had it that the house had originally been built by the silent-movie idol, screenwriter, and film director Francis X. Bushman—a Baltimore native. The Bushman Estate, as everyone called it, was huge: it had many rooms on three stories, including a spacious front foyer lined with glass-enclosed bookcases opening to a majestic curved staircase leading to the floor above. It looked like a movie set. The estate included an in-ground swimming pool, a large detached garage, and a substantial yard with gardens. They had paid $80,000 for the estate—a large amount for someone whose beginning salary at Hopkins was $31,000, but the couple knew that this was a good value; an estate like this back in California would cost hundreds of thousands of dollars back then. The swimming pool was a requirement of Susan: she had been extremely reluctant to leave her friends and move across country, so Adrienne and Stanley had promised that their new house would have a pool. Adrienne would decorate their new home with her usual pizzazz: modern art and sculptures would accentuate the beauty of the stately residence. It was a perfect home for entertaining, both on the spacious main floor and on the perfectly manicured lawn out back. They would have many parties there, and some years later Walter Benn Michael and Francis Ferguson—both Hopkins faculty—would be married there. Stanley made good use of the glass-enclosed bookcases: he filled them with remaindered copies of his own books and freely gave them as gifts to any guests who visited.

Soon after Stanley joined the faculty at Hopkins, the department made him their graduate placement officer. He had already distinguished himself as a placement officer at Berkeley, where he had served as co-chair of graduate placement with the celebrated American literature scholar Norman S. Grabo. Both men had disliked the antiwar protests at Berkeley and had disapproved of the propensity of many professors to cancel their classes and join their students in the protests. They believed deeply that their role was to professionalize students so that they would be able to compete well nationally for academic appointments or acceptance into other graduate programs. To that end, they would insist on vetting drafts of students' résumés and application letters, and they would provide grueling mock interviews for students on the job market, including critiques of the appropriateness of their clothing for a professional interview. Stanley continued these same practices at Johns Hopkins. The graduate program there was much smaller than the Berkeley program. The department graduated only three or four doctoral students each year, but because of the small size of the program, the quality of the faculty, and the personal attention from the professors, these graduates were exceedingly well trained. Part of that training entailed frequently attending events at the Tudor and Stuart Club. Many of the graduate students felt like spectators at gladiatorial combats during these sessions, but they learned much: not only the intellectual content of the talks but how to engage in (and survive) question-and-answer sessions. They also learned an important lesson about job talks. The department frequently brought speakers in with the intention of quietly considering them for possible appointments. All too often, these speakers made a serious strategic error: rather than simply present the research that had captured their passionate attention and stop there, many attempted to second-guess their audience by giving a talk that seemed directed at one of the Hopkins faculty in the audience, either to pay homage to him or to take issue with his research. Many invited speakers lost their chance for serious further consideration by making this mistake. The Hopkins graduate students in the audience benefited immensely from witnessing these faux pas, in that they graduated with a level of professional sophistication that many of their peers would only attain after serving as faculty members for some years, if at all.

Another factor that contributed to the success of the graduate program at the time was that everyone had a sense of being part of a tight-knit intellectual community—almost an extended family. Adrienne and Stanley would frequently hold parties at their house, so faculty and students socialized and came to know one another especially well—intellectually and personally. Adrienne was an excellent social hostess and skilled cook, and she loved to preside over social occasions. Stanley was a master event planner who relished the strategic challenges of organizing a large complex party more than he enjoyed attending them. Each Fish extravaganza—and there were many—was memorable to all who attended, and these events helped the Hopkins crowd bond and remain close for many years.

In the genteel, rarified atmosphere of Hopkins, the department in those days would rarely hold a formal meeting. Instead, department members would arrange to meet for lunch at the university's faculty club and discuss whatever business was at hand. Unlike the cutthroat proceedings of the Tudor and Stuart Club, the workings of these informal meetings were always quite subtle. Somebody would say something, like, "Well, colleagues, it would be nice if we did X." If no one objected, the issue was settled. There was never anything like calling the meeting to order, or invoking Robert's Rules of Order, or conducting a formal vote. On one occasion a newly hired faculty member attended his first such session and afterwards commented to Stanley, "I don't understand. Nothing happened." Amused, Stanley replied, "You don't get it. *Everything* just happened." The neophyte had missed the subtle workings of the group. This is not to suggest that the department did not have its share of politics or that the group always arrived at consensus, only that collectively the department members had developed a way of interacting that transcended or at least escaped the typical wrangling and infighting that characterizes so many English department meetings.

Stanley's career would take an important turn in 1976. He had developed an especially close relationship with Walter Benn Michaels. A brilliant literary theorist, Michaels had studied at the University of California at Santa Barbara and taught at both Berkeley and Hopkins, and Stanley would one day lure him to the University of Illinois at Chicago. Like Stanley, Michaels was an avid basketball player, not to mention an excellent tennis player. They both had formed a friendship with Kenneth S. Abraham, a professor at the University of Maryland's law school, which was located in Baltimore, not on the main campus in College Park. Abraham would go on to become one of the nation's most prominent legal scholars, specializing in torts and insurance law. The threesome would often play three-on-three games when they could find an opposing team. During these outings they found plenty of time to discuss intellectual issues, especially the intersections between legal and literary interpretation. To their surprise, they discovered many similarities in how interpretation worked in the two disciplines. Eventually they decided to co-teach a course on how interpretation works in literary and legal discourse. The University of Maryland's law school appointed Michaels and Stanley adjunct professors of law, and all three jointly developed the syllabus and co-taught the course, alternately teaching it first at the University of Maryland Law School and then at Hopkins. The seminar, titled Theories of Interpretation, drew substantial attention as a revolutionary experiment in interdisciplinary work. A Washington,

D.C., radio program even invited them on the air to describe the course and to answer questions from listeners.

While Michaels would publish some scholarly works on the subject, his real interests lay elsewhere. Stanley, however, had realized a dream. As a college student he had agonized over whether to attend law school or graduate school, and Adrienne had made it quite clear on numerous occasions that she preferred that he do the former. From time to time over the years he wondered if perhaps he shouldn't have studied law. Now he could achieve both goals: legal scholarship, especially concerning theories of legal interpretation, would become an important part of his scholarly output, and he would retain his position as adjunct professor of law at the University of Maryland Law School for years. He began to write for law reviews and to engage in the kinds of debates important to some scholars of the law. Over the years he would publish in such legal journals as the *Columbia Law Review, Duke Law Journal, Yale Law Journal, Stanford Law Review,* and the *University of Chicago Law Review,* and he would end his career as a chaired professor in the law school at Florida International University. One of the most famous of his debates was with Ronald Dworkin. Born and raised in Providence, Rhode Island, around the corner from where Stanley grew up, Dworkin was an eminent scholar of constitutional law. Trained at Harvard and Oxford, he taught at Yale and Oxford before becoming the Frank Henry Sommer Professor of Law at New York University. A prolific author, he is one of the most cited legal scholars of the twentieth century.

The boy who decades earlier employed his persuasive powers to argue himself out of being beaten up by bullies on the tough streets of Providence and who later honed those skills at the Tudor and Stuart Club and at hundreds of public presentations rarely met his match in a public, intellectual confrontation—that is, until the first time he locked horns with Dworkin. Stanley and two colleagues—Michael Fried and Walter Michaels—had been invited to a conference on interpretation at the University of Chicago. Among the presenters and respondents were such eminent scholars as Stanley Cavell, Julia Kristeva, Tom Mitchell, Gayatri Spivak, and Stephen Toulmin. Stanley had won the right to respond to a paper given by Dworkin. Respondents received advance copies of the papers they would respond to so that they could prepare their formal responses prior to the conference. Stanley believed that

Dworkin's reasoning was flawed, and he was prepared to demonstrate how. The distinguished legal scholar gave an erudite, articulate, and polished presentation. Unlike so many humanities professors, he did not speak from a written text; like a lawyer standing before the Supreme Court, he spoke in perfectly coherent paragraphs without referring to notes. He was impressive and imposing. After Dworkin finished, Stanley got up to offer his rejoinder. He was barely through his first sentence when the legal scholar interrupted him unceremoniously, seizing on one word in Stanley's sentence and forcing him into a defensive position. As Stanley began to explain his use of the word, Dworkin once again interrupted him, pouncing on another word and demanding that he clarify his point. With lightning-fast thrust and parry, Dworkin deftly cut him to ribbons. Stanley did his best to recover but failed. He had underestimated the power of this Oxford-trained debater. Never before—and never since—had he been so unable to gain the upper hand. Wounded and still experiencing Dworkin's onslaught, Stanley thought to himself, as he stood at the podium: I'm going to get this fucker—in print! And this is exactly what he did do in a series of articles, to which Dworkin responded. The so-called Fish-Dworkin debate attracted substantial scholarly attention and comment.

Briefly, Dworkin attempted to explain legal analysis and interpretation by using an analogy: a chain novel—that is, a story in which each successive chapter is composed by a different author. The author of each chapter will necessarily feel constrained by the tone, plot line, and character development worked out in previous chapters and will thus take pains to ensure that the new chapter coherently and organically arises from those that preceded it. Legal interpretation, Dworkin reasoned, similarly relies on decisions and interpretations that preceded it in a chain of successive decisions and interpretations. Like the chapter author, a conscientious judge will feel constrained by the chain of interpretations preceding the given legal problem at hand and will ensure that a new interpretation derives coherently from those that preceded it.

Not true, Fish argued. The interpreter far down the chain will feel no greater or lesser constraint than those early in the chain. In effect, rather than necessarily feeling constrained by prior interpretations, each new interpreter will re-create the facts and interpretations to justify the argument he or she feels compelled to make. The judge may draw on some precedents but not others—whatever better helps him or her rhetorically make the argument or justify the interpretation he or she thinks right.

This disagreement sparked a sustained debate between the two scholars in a succession of articles, some appearing in *Critical Inquiry*, about the nature of legal interpretation. Soon, other scholars joined the fray on one side or the other, creating a great deal of intellectual excitement over what was essentially a manifestation of the larger debate over epistemology between those taking an Enlightenment rationalist position and the postmodernist critique of that position.

A few years after Stanley's first confrontation with Dworkin—during the 1983–84 academic year, when Stanley was teaching at Columbia University as a visiting professor—Dworkin called him one Friday night and invited him to visit his seminar at New York University to discuss their differences about the workings of interpretation. The session was the following Monday—very little time for Stanley to prepare. "That's just typical Dworkin," he muttered to himself. Although he believed Dworkin was setting him up, he was not about to walk away from a challenge, especially one from his nemesis, the only scholar who was able to get the upper hand on him in a public debate.

When he arrived at the seminar that Monday, he discovered that a simple visit to someone's class had turned into a much bigger event: numerous faculty and other visitors had crowded into the classroom along with the students enrolled in the class. The air was thick with anticipation. The crowd clearly expected combat.

Dworkin began the session by taking the moral high ground: "Many have asked me why I have invited Professor Fish to this seminar given the fact that we have criticized each other so often recently in essays and various law reviews, most recently in the *Texas Law Review*. Well, of course, the answer is that there's no reason why a disagreement on intellectual matters should translate into a personal animosity between two scholars." Dworkin went on in this vein for some minutes, and then invited Stanley to speak. Stanley sauntered up to the head of the class and addressed the crowd: "Professor Dworkin is, of course, correct. There's absolutely no reason why a disagreement on an intellectual or disciplinary or theoretical matter should also turn into an animosity on a personal level between those involved in the disagreement." He paused for a moment before launching what he knew would be a stinging barb to Dworkin, who had during his time at Oxford adopted what some felt was an affected upper-crust British accent. "And besides, how could there be any animosity between two nice Jewish boys from Providence, Rhode Island?" This was the last thing that Dworkin wanted his colleagues and students to hear—and Stanley knew it. This was a calculated tactic on Stanley's part to level the playing field—after all, Dworkin had blindsided him by inviting him to what was set up to be an ambush. The tactic worked: Dworkin no longer had the upper hand psychologically. The rest of the session was a spirited but productive discussion. Ironically, years later Stanley would purchase an apartment in New York City a block or so from where Dworkin lived. They would run into one another from time to time in the neighborhood.

In 1976, the same year that Stanley and Walter Benn Michaels had begun to think about how theories of interpretation applied to legal theory, Temple University in Philadelphia invited Stanley to give a class on recent trends in literary theory—an invitation that would trigger a chain of events that would change his life forever. The class began as a graduate class with some faculty sitting in, but most of the graduate students left fairly early on in the term after they discovered that the revolutionary, counterintuitive theory of the time completely overturned conventional thought about epistemology, axiology, and literary theory. After attrition, the class consisted of only a handful of graduate students and faculty. Among the faculty was a linguist, Don Freeman; Barbara Harman, a scholar who would write a respected book on the works of George Herbert and who would spend most of her career at Wellesley College; and an Americanist who had earned her PhD at Yale a few years after Stanley had: Jane Tompkins.

By that year, the revolution in thought about literary criticism and epistemology in general was raging full force, capturing the imagination of many intellectuals throughout the academy. Those who paid attention to the new trends felt that they had become part of a sweeping movement that overturned centuries-old ways of understanding how knowledge is produced. Tompkins was aware that something exciting was happening in intellectual history, but she was not yet familiar with exactly what it was. Feeling that she was in a bit of an intellectual rut and curious about the new trends in literary criticism, she had signed up to sit in on Stanley's class. She had heard that he was at the forefront of these trends, and she was eager to learn what she could. Her initial impression was not positive. He seemed brash, arrogant, and full of himself. He informed the class that everything they had learned about reading and the relationship of reader to a text was wrong but that he would soon set them all straight. She was horrified. Who did this short, chubby, ill-dressed, cigar-smoking bully think he was? Her aversion, however, was counterbalanced by her fascination, first for the material they were reading and discussing, and then for this forceful personality that was guiding them through the intricacies of postmodern thought. The course was rigorous. He assigned an overwhelming number of difficult theoretical texts to read, and keeping up with the assignments was difficult even for the faculty in the class. At first she resisted the material, thinking it was nonsense, some fleeting trend. She would argue with him in class, suggesting that some of his claims were outrageous and untenable. But despite her resistance, she forced herself to persevere. She took pains to read the material carefully, and even read supplemental texts on the side. "I'm going to master this material," she promised herself. Then, one morning while showering she had an epiphany. All of the seemingly disparate parts of the theoretical material they had been reading suddenly seemed to fit together to form a coherent account. "*Now* I get what it's all about," she almost shouted. The intellectual rush was exhilarating. At that moment, her life had changed.

The rest of the semester was an exciting intellectual high. She had never felt such intellectual excitement in her life. Her years at Yale had been sedate in comparison. No one at Yale seemed to get overly passionate about intellectual work; that would have been considered unseemly: "proper" ladies and gentlemen do not emote, especially about intellectual matters. Stanley, in contrast, brought a high level of passion to his work every moment he stood in front of the class. Before long, the boundaries between intellectual and sexual excitement began to blur. He may be brash, she thought, but he's not so bad after all. And, boy, does he know his stuff. He's brilliant!

Stanley and Jane both felt the sparks between them—intellectual and sexual—but they repressed these feelings—at least for the time being. Both were married; they lived in very different worlds; they traveled in very different circles. He was a Jewish boy from the rough streets of Providence; she was a WASP from a very proper middle-class family. He was loud and brash; she was raised in a family where no one ever raised their voice—ever. He was a jet-setting intellectual at a prestigious private institution; she was an emerging scholar at a modest public university. They were an unlikely couple, but the flames ignited during that course at Temple kept burning even after they had parted at semester's end.

That December at the convention of the Modern Language Association (MLA), Jane and Stanley would meet in the hotel lounge and enjoy a drink together. It was clear to them both that the flame was burning ever so brightly, but the timing was not right: Stanley was secretly involved with a faculty member at another university, and he did not want to complicate his life even further. He was a bad boy—and knew it. But he needed intimate time with someone who would not quarrel with him at every moment. He needed time away from Adrienne; he had realized that being home with Adrienne was like being home with his mother—constant bickering, endless recriminations, and ceaseless verbal combat. And besides, this was the 1970s: in the academic world, everyone seemed to be sleeping with someone other than their spouse—colleagues' spouses, graduate students, even undergraduates. It was the tail end of the free-love sexual revolution that began in the 1960s, and the concept of sexual harassment was not yet generally known. The sexual tension was palpable when they left each other after enjoying cocktails at the MLA convention.

Stanley had been chosen to serve as an instructor that summer of 1976 at the School of Criticism and Theory Summer Institute at the University of California at Irvine. Murray Krieger, a prominent literary critic on the Irvine faculty, had founded the institute the year before, and even though it was only in its second year of existence, it had already become prestigious—*the* place to teach if you were a major figure in the field, *the* place to attend if you wanted someday to be a major figure yourself. Joining Stanley as instructors that year were Krieger, Leonard Meyers, Edward Said, and Barbara Herrnstein Smith.

Adrienne and Stanley were delighted to spend part of the summer in sunny California. They rented a chic house on Balboa Island, an exclusive, man-made island off of Newport Beach. Balboa was a beautiful resort location for the beautiful people. Murray Krieger had found them an exquisite—and very expensive—house with a stunning view of the bay, and Adrienne, Susan, and their then two dogs would make a vacation of their time there. Jane Tompkins and her colleague Barbara Harman had also rented a cottage on Balboa Island. They were on fire from their introduction to literary theory in Stanley's class at Temple that fall and had signed up to take several classes at the institute, including his. Jane was on fire in other ways as well.

The intellectual electricity of the institute was palpable. Continental philosophy had thrown into question the intellectual community's most cherished assumptions, and a group of faculty had gathered for six weeks of intensive exposure to these new ideas. Inside and outside the formal classes, the air was thick with debate, discussion, and contestation. Participants ate, drank, and studied together. If Stanley's course at Temple was the height of intellectual intensity, the institute was that same intensity cubed. Decades later he would characterize that summer as the most intense intellectual experience he had ever had, even more intense than Hopkins because of the compression of time. The intense intellectual atmosphere had a sexual charge, felt by many of the participants. They were studying sexy, avant-garde theory presented by some of the nation's most high-powered scholars, and for six weeks they all spent their days and half the evenings in each other's company—dining, drinking, debating, discussing theory.

On the final evening before everyone would depart for their respective institutions, the institute organizers held a concluding party. Everyone was exhausted from the sheer intensity of the last several weeks, but no one wanted it to end. They stood around sipping cocktails, snacking on hors d'oeuvres, and recapping their weeks at the institute. Jane and Stanley stood in a quiet corner, cocktails in hand. They made small talk for a while, and then suddenly, as if on cue, they abandoned their drinks and stealthily slipped out for a long stroll on the beach. They knew then that they were hopelessly in love with each other. There was no turning back. They would deal with the consequences later.

Early that September of 1976, Stanley was scheduled to attend the thirty-sixth annual conference of the English Institute, which was being held in New York City that year. The English Institute was very prestigious. It sponsored an annual three-day conference focusing on cutting-edge theory and scholarship, presented by the most eminent scholars of the time. Being invited to give a talk was a sign that you had arrived. The conference papers were compiled each year in a volume and published as a book, often by Johns Hopkins University Press. Stanley always attended, whether he was speaking or not. On a hot, humid day late in August, he picked up the phone and dialed Jane. "Will you be going to the English Institute?" he asked. Jane wasn't sure she was going to attend, nor was she sure it was a good idea. "Why don't you come? It will be fun," he asked. She made no promises. Stanley had broken off his romance with the woman he had been seeing and felt unencumbered.

He arrived at the English Institute and sat through the first day of presentations. They were impressive, but he was distracted. Every time the auditorium door opened, he immediately looked over his shoulder to see who was entering the room. Each time, he was disappointed. Clearly, Jane was not there. He had almost given up hope when on the second day Jane suddenly made an appearance. She looked as beautiful as ever. They greeted each other warmly and settled down to hear a talk presented by Marxist critic (and a future colleague of theirs at Duke) Fredric Jameson. Ten minutes into the talk, they could feel the sexual tension surging between them. The speaker seemed to drone on, and after a moment they could no longer hear him. Suddenly, without a word, they got up in the middle of the talk and left together. They were absent from much of the rest of the conference.

What followed was a nine-month clandestine relationship managed through an elaborate set of furtive strategies, complicated prevarications, and surreptitious meetings. As academics, they had more opportunities than most people to disappear periodically without suspicion. They made ample use of that advantage. This period was at once exciting, frightening, and hair-raising. They both knew that their affair could not continue in this manner indefinitely, but they were caught up in the exhilaration of the moment and their love for one each. Their life at the time was one of controlled chaos—barely controlled.

Throughout the entire affair, they both were riven with guilt. Jane was married to an instructor of religious studies at Haverford College, Dan Larkin, who was working toward his PhD at the University of Chicago. This was her second marriage, and it had not been faring well. She was not especially happy at home, but neither was she ready to divorce. Despite the bickering at home with Adrienne, Stanley was thoroughly devoted to his daughter and worried constantly about what effect a divorce would have on her. Yet, he was very much in love—probably for the first time in his life. Finally, one day in April of 1977 he did the right thing: he sat down with Adrienne and told her as gently as he could about the affair. She was justifiably outraged, and she made sure Stanley knew it. She felt utterly betrayed. How dare he! She had supported him through college and graduate school, typed his manuscripts, presided over his countless parties, kept his house, cared for their daughter and dogs. What chutzpah! She immediately threw him out of the house. Jane had already told her husband about the affair, but they were still living together—they had an understanding.

Jane was vacillating about leaving her marriage. She felt conflicted, tormented. Stanley had agreed to call her at a prearranged time that Sunday. Impatient, he hopped in his car and drove the hundred miles or so to Fairmount Park, near Philadelphia. When he arrived, he found a nearby phone booth, struggled to find a dime, and rang her up. It was like a bad movie—melodramatic, overplayed, and somewhat unbelievable. Jane answered the phone and was stunned to discover that Stanley was a block or two away. An avid jogger, she told her husband that she going out for a run. She quickly donned her running shoes and waved good-bye to her husband. She sprinted down the street, leapt into Stanley's car, and they sped away. She never returned.

They ran away. Just like in the movies.

The timing was not good for anyone. Jane's husband, Dan, was in the middle of exams during his first year of law school. His dissertation in religious studies had not been approved, so he had decided to switch careers and obtain a law degree. Jane was desperately trying to stay focused on her teaching obligations at Temple. Adrienne was building her own career besides keeping house. And Stanley had committed to countless projects, all vying for his attention, not to mention his teaching duties at Hopkins.

The next few months were difficult for Stanley and Jane. They first needed somewhere to live. Until they could find a suitable apartment of their own, they stayed a few days with Stanley's colleague and good friend Stephen Orgel, and then they stayed at the flat of one of Stanley's junior colleagues, Barry Weller, who was away at the time. Stanley immediately began to experience a crisis of conscience. The guilt and anxiety were overwhelming; he walked around in a trancelike state. "What have I done?" he asked himself repeatedly. They had been married nearly two decades; it seemed a lifetime. On an impulse, he decided that Jane and he should get out of town—drive to Florida. It was late in June of 1977, perhaps the worst time of year to be in hot, sticky Florida. Stanley had no money because Adrienne had understandably cleaned out their bank accounts, so he borrowed $500 from the department secretary. They slid into his white 1970 Mercedes coupe and sped down Interstate 95. He desperately needed to restore his equilibrium, and he felt that a long automobile trip would be therapeutic—just as the long trip he had taken in 1974 had helped him overcome a brief bout of depression.

From the beginning, the trip was a comedy of errors, though it certainly did not seem comedic to the lovebirds. It was punctuated by a series of mishaps. The Mercedes, which had performed admirably for years, repeatedly gave them trouble. Their first night in a motel was quite unpleasant: everything there seemed to go wrong. Then, as they approached the exit to Savannah, Georgia, they ran out of gas—a mere half mile from the exit and its several gas stations. "What next?" Stanley exclaimed in his typically animated voice. He pulled the coupe to the shoulder of the highway and trudged the half mile or so to a gas station, where he purchased a gas can and a gallon of gas. In the course of sloshing gas into his disabled Mercedes, his designer sunglasses slipped unnoticed from his pocket.

Travel worn, the couple decided to stay the night in Savannah. They toured the historic downtown area and walked hand in hand along the waterfront. Savannah was quaint, beautiful, and delightful. The town was peaceful and relaxing. Suddenly, for no apparent reason, Stanley's spirits lifted for the first time in months. The stress seemed to melt away. He began to feel better about everything—about his decision to leave Adrienne and to take up with Jane. His decision had been painful—and hurtful to others—but it was the right thing to do.

The rest of the trip was much more pleasurable. They arrived in Florida and stayed in a condo that Stanley's parents owned. Max and Ida were aghast at what their son had done, though they were not in Florida at the time, and his aunt and uncle, who lived in Florida, were also appalled at Stanley's behavior, although they were very hospitable to both Jane and Stanley. The lovebirds managed to have an enjoyable time. They decompressed, rested, gained their energy back, and reconfirmed to themselves that they had made the right decision.

They eventually needed to make their way back to their daily realities up north. Reluctantly, they fueled up the coupe and headed north on Interstate 95. As they motored through Savannah, Stanley recognized where he had run out of gas. He hoped to retrieve his sunglasses, so he pulled to the shoulder of the road and sprinted across to the southbound side of the highway. There they were, just where he had dropped them. They had been crushed, undoubtedly run over. He picked them up gently and stared at them for a moment, attempting to interpret their meaning. Did the shattered glasses symbolize his shattered marriage? Was it some omen about what was to come? Both? He saw his reflection in the glass. Had he run over the glasses himself? Had he inadvertently destroyed them? Uncharacteristically, he had no answers.

With the pall of their transgression behind them, the couple took their time on the return trip. They visited friends, first in Charleston, then in Richmond. Normalcy—or some semblance of it—was finally returning to their lives. They were ready to start their new lives together.

They decided they would find an apartment in Baltimore and that Jane would commute to her job in Philadelphia until they could find appointments in the same department. They both hoped that Hopkins would hire Jane, but that was not to be. They searched extensively for an acceptable apartment in Baltimore and had trouble finding one they both liked. They finally found a very nice two-bedroom, two-bath apartment on the ninth floor of a new building at 4100 North Charles Street, and they set up their home there. The eleven-hundred-square-foot apartment looked into a bank of stately trees, and the residents in the building had access to a swimming pool. Eventually, the couple bought a modest house on Southway near the university, a three-story house with an attractive sunroom and a brick patio. Jane had the entire third floor as her study. In fact, in all the houses and apartments they would live in together, she would have the more spacious study, mostly because Stanley did not care where he worked; he could write just as well in a cramped nook as a grand study.

Jane had entered academe's fast lane, the same fast lane that Stanley had been moving in for some time. They had become the preeminent power couple—celebrity academics, royalty in the world of English studies. When they made an appearance at the MLA convention or other conferences, other scholars and graduate students would point and whisper proudly to one another, "That's Stanley Fish and Jane Tompkins," as if the sheer act of being able to recognize them somehow catapulted them into a special class. At the many cocktail receptions held in the evenings during the MLA convention, people would conspire to be introduced to the couple. Spectators would crowd the room when they presented papers, and sometimes even when they were simply attending a session. After all, you never knew when Stanley would respond to a paper—as he did frequently—and the sparks would fly. Stanley's annual schedule was unimaginably grueling to many faculty. He would jet from university to university, giving workshops, papers, and presentations, both in the United States and abroad. He was in great demand and knew it, so he pushed the boundaries of what universities would pay to bring in a humanities professor to speak. Whatever he was offered by a university, he would demand more—and he usually got it. The host who invited him would scramble to meet his fee, asking various campus departments and entities to contribute to the event until the requisite fee had been collected. Throughout his career he must have visited almost every notable university in every state in the union.

Jane's newfound celebrity was exhilarating to her. She suddenly found herself in demand, and she began producing feminist and other theoretical scholarship and giving talks. What she hated was the weekly grind of her schedule as a commuting scholar. For the first few years she would commute to Temple two to three times a week, taking the train and subway. She would sometimes stay overnight at her parents' house in the suburbs or at a friend's apartment. When in Baltimore, she would join Stanley and socialize with the various friends, colleagues, and visiting scholars in the Hopkins circle. Then she would leave this genteel world to board the train and travel back to what seemed like another planet: the gritty urban campus of Temple. Week in and week out she negotiated the trains and subways, her teaching schedule at Temple, her own scholarly obligations, and her many engagements—both academic and social—with Stanley and his crowd. She maintained this geographical schizophrenia valiantly year after year, but it took its toll. She felt worn down by the relentless demand of her obligations; the fast lane was no easy lane to navigate, especially when you had feet in two different worlds, especially when you were married to Stanley Fish.

Despite their lobbying, the couple was unsuccessful in garnering sufficient support from the Hopkins faculty for an appointment for Jane.

They liked and respected her, and they accepted her as a friend and scholar, but they felt that she did not yet have the academic record that would warrant an appointment at Hopkins. It fell to Jane's good friend and fellow Americanist, Sharon Cameron, to deliver the bad news: the department had conducted a formal review of her credentials to determine her viability as a candidate for an appointment, and it had become clear that she did not fit the profile of a Hopkins scholar. A number of institutional and disciplinary prejudices likely contributed to this assessment. Jane did not yet have a single-authored scholarly monograph; much of her published scholarship was nontraditional rather than traditional literary analysis; she had spent her career so far teaching not at an elite private institution like Hopkins but at an urban public institution; and, of course, she was seen first as the woman that Stanley had run away with rather than as the emerging major scholar that she would soon become. This decision was heartbreaking to them both: it meant that Stanley would eventually have to leave his academic utopia and that Jane would have to be torn between two worlds until they could find appointments together somewhere.

In 1978 Hopkins made Stanley a chaired professor: the William Kenan Jr. Professor of English and Humanities. Also that year, the University of California Press published his *The Living Temple: George Herbert and Catechizing*. In it, he adopts a familiar strategy: he explains that there are two seemingly irreconcilable camps of critics among Herbert scholars, and he shows that they can in fact be reconciled by a fresh understanding of what the poet was attempting to accomplish; in doing so, he would once again demonstrate how formalist approaches to literary texts were inadequate. The critical literature has in effect created two Herberts, he argues—one is the careful craftsman who is calm, resolute, and methodical; the other is unruly, restless, and unstable. Stanley posits that Herbert's poetry can be both orderly and unstable at the same time. It is the tension between these two states that makes the poetry great; adopting one perspective over the other does injustice to the work by disguising its complexity. The catechism embodies this tension, in that it is simultaneously structured and open: the catechist asks structured questions; the initiate gropes insecurely toward mastery of the knowledge. This model of the catechism is also a metaphor for the workings of the author/reader relationship: one embodies the stability of a prior intention; the other embodies the realization of that intention. *The Living Temple* was generally well reviewed but just as controversial as any of Stanley's works because it challenged everyone's long-held assumptions. It would further solidify his reputation as a major literary critic.

In 1980 Stanley directed a National Endowment for the Humanities Summer Seminar on Milton and Critical Theory, and Harvard University Press published *Is There a Text in This Class? Interpretive Communities and the Sources of Authority*. It contains four new essays and twelve previously published works. Together, they lay out his understanding of how interpretation works. This book is important because he self-reflectively changes his own theoretical perspective on the subject. He once saw the author, text, and reader as competing to constrain interpretation; he now sees all three as being constituted by interpretation—a distinctly poststructuralist nuance. *Is There a Text in This Class?* became one of his best-known works and was assigned as required reading in many graduate courses in literary theory across the nation. It also further fueled the animosity that more conventional critics had both toward the enfant terrible and toward postmodern theory generally. Works such as this completely unsettled their comfortable, unquestioned understanding of how reading works; it turned their intellectual world upside down. Stanley dedicated the book to Ida and Max, and he credited Kenneth Abraham and Walter Michaels with having helped him work out many of the intricacies of interpretation, not only during their co-taught classes but at social engagements and on the basketball court. He also declared that Jane Tompkins had inspired him and gave meaning to his life.

That same year, 1980, Stanley and Adrienne were legally divorced. It was a relief to them both. They would stay in touch over the years, and on occasion Adrienne, Jane, Susan, and Stanley would find themselves dining together for one reason or another, but Adrienne would remain bitter throughout her life. She never forgave him. She would go on to be successful in her own right. In 1986 she would open up an art gallery and bookstore in San Francisco called 871 Fine Arts specializing in books on contemporary art, both new and out of print. The shop also sells drawings, paintings, prints, and sculptures. It was a huge success, a favorite destination of many in the arts and literati circles of San Francisco.

The year 1980 was especially important to Jane for another reason: she was invited to be a featured speaker at a special conference on literary theory held in Orono, Maine—her first invitation as a major scholar in her own right. Stanley would accompany Jane to the high-powered conference. A number of important scholars were in attendance, including Gerald Graff, an Americanist and literary theorist. As a fellow Americanist, Graff knew Jane but had never met Stanley. Jane and Graff were on the same panel together, and Stanley sat through the session in the audience. During the question-and-answer session to Graff's paper, a number of more radically deconstructionist scholars in the audience attacked Graff viciously. His book *Literature against Itself* had come out the year before, and some regarded it as conservative and retrograde. Graff was an excellent scholar, but he was not always adept at handling frontal assaults. He was being badly beaten up by the crowd. Finally, Stanley had had enough. He found Graff's argument to be cogent and well argued and the attacks unwarranted and petty. He stood up authoritatively, and in his commanding—some would say *imperious*—voice said, "Now, wait just one minute. You are all acting as if he is the only person in the world who holds any of these views when in fact the viewpoints he is presenting are taken seriously by an enormous number of serious scholars, and we should take them seriously." He went on to engage the detractors and defend the perspective that Graff was attempting to further. After the session, Jane, Stanley, and Graff retired to the lounge for cocktails. Despite their several philosophical differences, the three of them, from that moment on, would become the best of friends, and many years later as a dean at the University of Illinois at Chicago, Stanley would lure Graff away from the University of Chicago to become one of his associate deans.

Despite the difficulties of their life in a commuting relationship, Jane and Stanley were exceedingly happy together. On August 7 of 1982, they married. It was a simple affair held in their home. Thirty-two guests attended, including Susan, both sets of parents, Stanley's two brothers, and several of their friends from Hopkins. Walter Benn Michaels was there, as was the award-winning Americanist and poet John Irwin, and the art historian and critic Michael Fried—three of their closest friends. The university chaplain and noted civil rights activist Chester L. Wickwire performed the ceremony. A high school friend of Jane's, Bob Sherman, a military analyst and weapons expert in Washington, D.C., played a trumpet voluntary as Jane processed down the stairs to be wed. At the reception and catered dinner Susan offered a toast: she raised her glass and said simply, "I hope it lasts!" They would honeymoon on Block Island, a popular tourist destination off the south coast of Rhode Island.

The word got out in the early 1980s that the couple were unhappy with their commuter marriage and that they might be amenable to being lured away to another institution. Several universities hastened to attract them. Columbia offered them both yearlong appointments for the 1983–84 academic year—another "look-see" arrangement—and they accepted. Like Hopkins, Columbia's English department had a stellar reputation and was quite exclusive, but unlike Hopkins, it did not have the same tight-knit, intimate, collegial atmosphere. It was not a place where lively relationships flourished, and the couple would find this fact quite dispiriting. The department was hopelessly caught up in its own self-image and its own byzantine internal politics; it was a distinctly unfriendly atmosphere. Nevertheless, Jane and Stanley loved New York City (Jane was born and raised there; she had the city in her blood), and they liked Columbia as an institution. In fact, as Stanley spent increasingly more time in Columbia's law school, he found the atmosphere there to be much more amiable and welcoming. Jane was assigned the office that for many years had been occupied by the great Lionel Trilling. Despite the unfriendly English department, she hoped that Columbia would work out for them both, but she increasingly felt that she was not being well treated by some members of the faculty.

The couple presumed from the start that Columbia would make Stanley an offer—and they eventually did; the question was whether they would also make Jane an offer. Her first authored book of scholarship, *Sensational Designs*, had been accepted by Oxford University Press but was not out yet. It would solidify her reputation as a scholar in her own right. She had published two very well received edited collections of scholarly works—*Reader-Response Criticism: From Formalism to Post-Structuralism* (1980), and *James' "Turn of the Screw" and Other Tales: Collection of Critical Essays* (1971)—but anthologies do not command the respect that single-authored scholarly monographs do, especially in elite institutions. One day the premier Americanist in the Columbia English department, Ann Douglas, asked Jane to lunch and informed Jane that she was just not the caliber of scholar that Columbia usually appointed, so she would not be receiving an offer for a full-time appointment. Jane was astonished, not only by the nearsightedness of the assessment but by the gall of her rival. (Jane had recently published an essay in *Glyph* that was a full-bore critique of Douglas's work.) Douglas then smiled and informed her that she had been thinking for some years about reducing her own appointment to half time, and she graciously—or mischievously—offered to allow Jane to share her appointment. Jane was stunned. She was already a player on the national scene and would soon be even more so once her book was out. She politely declined.

Understandably, the news was a great disappointment to the couple. In an unusually generous gesture, Columbia allowed Stanley to have an entire year to make his decision to come there while he and Jane attempted to find another appointment nearby for Jane. Fortunately, Jane secured a one-year visiting appointment—a "look-see" of her own—at the City University of New York (CUNY) Graduate Center. She taught two courses and rented a small flat in the West Village, sometimes known as "Little Bohemia" because it was a mecca for artists of all types. She loved both her classes and her flat on Morton Street. She would spend countless hours in the coffee shop at the top of the building of the CUNY Graduate Center engaged in intellectual discussion and debate with her colleagues and students. She held court. She was the queen of the coffee shop. She felt at home; this is what professorial life should be like. She just loved it.

The CUNY students were engaged and enthusiastic. Many were non-traditional students in terms of age, so they were mature and serious about their work. She found it fun to teach people who were genuinely interested in the subject rather than taking a class because it is a ticket to somewhere else. In those days, it was quite common to smoke in classrooms on American campuses. Many professors would smoke a pipe while lecturing, while their students would light up cigarettes. Jane smoked pencil-thin cigars. The students admired and tried to emulate Jane. Some wanted to live the life of a high-powered, feminist literary critic, and they associated doing literary theory with smoking little cigars. Soon, students began bringing the same thin cigars to class.

When the time came, the department faculty voted to offer her an appointment. Circumstances could not have been more perfect: she would teach at CUNY, and Stanley would teach nearby at Columbia. Finally, they would be together—or at least close by.

In his typically bold manner, Stanley called the Columbia provost, Jonathan Cole, and informed him that Jane would likely be accepting an offer at CUNY and that he would likely accept the offer at Columbia, but he had a suggestion to sweeten the pot: he wanted also to be appointed department chair. Cole did not skip a beat. He pointed out that Stanley was new to Columbia and did not know the lay of the land. "That's precisely why you *should* appoint me chair," he replied. "What's needed here is someone who is not burdened by Columbia's stultifying past—a leader who wasn't Lionel Trilling's former student or an acolyte of Quentin Anderson, someone who would come in with a fresh perspective and lead the department into modern times." The provost seemed unconvinced, but the point became moot within a week or two: the CUNY provost refused to approve Jane's appointment. Despite the vote of the faculty, the department chair very much opposed hiring a feminist, deconstructionist like Jane, and she reportedly went directly to the provost and made an impassioned over-my-dead-body speech. Jane's heart was broken. Everything had seemed so perfect. The stars were aligned, but it was not to be.

The CUNY provost's decision was quite unpopular in the English department, where Jane had won many friends and admirers, including the accomplished Miltonist Joseph Wittreich and the linguist Samuel Levin. And she was exceedingly popular with the students, as she was at Columbia. She was a charismatic teacher and mentor. Outraged at their department chair's actions, the faculty held a vote of no confidence in the chair, who was subsequently removed from office. For whatever reason—some suggested politics (Jane, after all, was a "radical" in some people's view)—the provost refused to change his mind. Her friend and colleague Sam Levin called her to break the bad news, and she instantly burst into tears. This was the only job she had every passionately wanted, but it was not to be. She was crestfallen.

Once it was clear that the CUNY position was dead in the water, Stanley turned down the Columbia offer, and the couple decided to redouble their efforts to find appointments together somewhere. Sensing an opportunity, Rice University immediately began wooing the couple. They invited them to campus and wined and dined them lavishly, eventually making them extremely handsome offers. Meanwhile, Duke University was also trying to lure them. Frank Lentricchia, who had joined the

Duke faculty only the year before, spearheaded the recruitment effort. A scholar of American literature and film, Lentricchia had earned his PhD from Duke in 1966. As a fellow Americanist, he knew Jane's work well; they had become friends over the years, and he was determined to bring her to Duke. In the eyes of some, the Duke English department in those days was a relatively undistinguished department with seemingly little aspiration to become a nationally prominent department, and Lentricchia, at the provost's urging, set out to change that. He engineered a campaign to recruit not only Jane and Stanley but Fredric Jameson and his wife, Susan Willis, an Americanist. Lentricchia wrote to Jane and asked if they would be interested in considering Duke. He had heard from some of his contacts at Rice that the Houston-based university was actively courting her. Jane immediately said yes.

Some weeks later, Jane and Stanley were in Baltimore sitting at the kitchen table when the phone rang. Stanley answered the phone, and the speaker introduced herself as Ernestine Friedl, the dean of arts and sciences at Duke. After trading a few niceties, the dean said, "I'm calling to extend an offer to you and Professor Tompkins to join our faculty as senior professors in the English department." Stunned, Stanley replied, "You mean you're calling to invite us to become *candidates* for senior positions." "No," she replied. "I'm calling to make you the offers!" Jane and Stanley were speechless.

Duke had a new academic administration, and it wanted to greatly enhance the university's national prominence. While its professional schools—particularly the medical school, the law school, and the divinity school—were highly ranked in their fields, its academic programs did not enjoy the same stellar reputation, so the administration set out to recruit a number of high-profile professors. Realizing that recruiting a large number of prominent senior professors in the sciences would be too costly, they decided to concentrate first on the humanities. The administration asked each department in the humanities to compile a list of scholars that they would like to be able to hire were funds to become available. Lentricchia had made sure that the English department's list contained Jane and Stanley. Although the administration did not make it clear in advance, it regarded the list compiled by a department as a declaration that it approved the hiring of anyone on the list—in other words, that no vetting process was necessary were the funds to become available. This is why the dean could make offers without having had Jane and Stanley on campus for interviews and to give papers and attend the usual battery of meetings. When word leaked out that they and other scholars like Fred Jameson had been made offers, some faculty members became outraged, construing this action as a subversion of the faculty's right to have a say in who is hired. The administration pointed out that they had already solicited input from the faculty by requesting an official wish list from the departments.

With offers in hand, Jane and Stanley decided to visit the campus. Unlike the smooth, collegial visit to Rice, the visit to Duke was terribly mismanaged. Although not required to do so, they chose to give papers and to go through the usual hoops. Stanley gave a talk on Milton's "Lycidas" rather than on a theoretical subject so that no one in the rather conventional department would feel threatened. Jane, who was traveling separately, arrived the next day and was picked up at the airport not by a dignitary, either in the administration or the faculty, but by a junior female faculty member. Later that night she met with a few women in the department who turned out to be in various degrees of disaffection from the department because they felt that it treated women horribly. They passionately recounted tales of various departmental transgressions. She had the distinct feeling of huddling together in the servants' quarters on some big plantation. Their narrative about the department and its treatment of women seemed borne out by the fact that there didn't seem to be much attention paid to Jane's part of the visit. She gave a talk that was an attack on Perry Miller's racism in his *Errand into the Wilderness*. The conservative Americanists in the department clearly did not like her talk, and not a single person was gracious enough to say anything positive about her paper. When she arrived at what was billed as a meeting with students, she found that no one had come to meet her, not even an escort. She sat alone for fifteen minutes in a lounge dominated by a huge moose head and musty oversize leather chairs. An imposing sign on the door announced, "Faculty Only." Furious, she had made up her mind to leave when the head of women's studies stopped in to say hello on her way to an all-day feminist-Marxist conference being held on campus. Insulted by how she was being treated, Jane immediately decided to skip her scheduled meetings and instead accompany her new friend to the conference. Jane was offended by the old-boy culture of the department and by the complete dismissal of her by what one feminist called the "bunch of old, potbellied guys who rule the department."

When they returned to Baltimore, Jane was adamant: "Forget about Duke. I will never join such a retrograde department." Meanwhile Duke's new provost, Philip Griffiths, who was part of the new-guard administration attempting to change Duke's culture and reputation, got wind of how terribly Jane had been treated. Presumably, Frank Lentricchia had complained to Dean Friedl about the department's bad behavior, and the dean had in turn alerted the provost. The provost was incensed. He immediately called Jane, apologized profusely, and begged her to allow him to sponsor another campus visit. "We'll do it right this time," he promised. Jane hesitated and then reluctantly agreed.

Jane did have another campus visit, and this time it was done right— with all the deference, recognition, and respect befitting someone who had become part of academe's favorite power couple. Jane immediately struck up a friendship with the provost's wife, Taffy, a neurologist, and they would become lifelong friends. Although the university did its best to atone for its mistreatment of Jane, she was still not persuaded that Duke would be a friendly place for her—or for any female faculty. The old-boy white patriarchy seemed hopelessly entrenched, and the horror stories of widespread sexism that she had heard from the few female faculty there suggested that this department was not likely to change in the foreseeable future.

Jane and Stanley now faced a dilemma. Rice had treated them superbly, but the fit was not right: Rice concentrated mostly on undergraduate education; Jane and Stanley felt more at home in large graduate research institutions. Stanley felt that he could make a real difference at Duke, and there was a tacit understanding that he would be made department chair after he had been there for a year. Yet, the list of reasons not to go to Duke was long. Complicating matters was the fact that Vanderbilt University had begun to make overtures to them. They kept debating the pros and cons for nearly two months. Then, one day, they were visiting Providence for a family event, and as they sat in their hotel room discussing their future, Jane repeated for the umpteenth time that the Duke department was "horrible." Stanley locked eyes with her and said, "Okay, Jane, *then I will change it.*" Jane knew instantly that if anyone could, it would be Stanley. At that moment they agreed to go to Duke.

Once back at Hopkins, Stanley told his friend and colleague Ron Paulson that he had accepted a position at Duke University. Paulson stared at him incredulously and retorted, "Stanley, people like us don't go to places like *that!*" He meant that no one willingly trades a coveted position at an elite university like Hopkins—academic utopia—for an appointment at an unremarkable southern institution like Duke. Duke, especially the leadership at the time, might have aspirations to join the same league as Vanderbilt and Emory—and in fact one day would—but then in the mid-1980s it was not considered an especially desirable institution by the elite. With the exception of the novelist Reynolds Price, there were few nationally prominent scholars in the Duke English department. The department did have a sizable contingent of American literature scholars and could boast of being the sponsor of the *Journal of American Literature*, the official MLA forum of American literature scholarship, but few thought of this as a particularly impressive department. Stanley smiled and replied to Paulson, "Wait and see. I will put them on the map."

Chapter 5

The Department That Soared— and Then Plummeted

The Duke University English department in 1985 was respectable, but it had a long way to go if it was to rival institutions like Yale or Hopkins or Columbia. The administration at Duke had taken the first steps toward building a first-rate humanities presence by recruiting Stanley, Jane, Fred Jameson, and Susan Willis, but it would be up to Stanley and Jameson to follow through. Stanley would, and with a level of success no one could ever have predicted.

Well before accepting their positions and before Jane was fully on board with moving to North Carolina, Jameson and Stanley had had a long discussion on the phone, asking many questions: Is this the right thing to do? Should we go to a place like Duke? Can we make it work? Will the faculty really let us put them on the map? Or will there be too much resistance? Academic faculty often resent "outsiders" coming into their department or college and attempting to make substantive changes. By the end of the phone call, they had resolved to give it a try, to attempt to launch this promising department into the big leagues.

Some faculty members did resent the administration for hiring the foursome. They felt that the administration had been heavy-handed and should have allowed the faculty to vote on whether to appoint each candidate separately. One faculty member lambasted the dean during a chance encounter at the train station for not respecting proper process. Another approached Stanley when he first arrived and said in a mournful tone, "You'll never be able to do anything here." The first was laboring under the values of the old regime and was a direct recipient of the perks of that regime. Like others, he feared the potential loss of his own position of privilege and unearned departmental largesse. The second was sympathetic and had been a victim of the old regime, but he had succumbed to a feeling of resignation and hopelessness about the plight of the department and the impossibility of constructive change. He was jaded.

Stanley bided his time. The term of the current department chair, the Renaissance scholar George Williams, would be over in a year, and the tacit understanding was that Stanley would then succeed him. He used his first year to network with his new colleagues and to win many of them over, and when he did take over in 1986 he had won substantial support among the faculty.

The minute he became chair, he began a relentless effort to transform the department into the most prominent English department in the nation. The first order of business was to improve the departmental climate. Unlike Hopkins or even Berkeley, the Duke English department seemed to lack cohesiveness and community; it was not the kind of tight-knit circle of friends and colleagues that a well-functioning department should be. Some felt that it also suffered from a collective inferiority complex. While the institution perceived itself as competing with Vanderbilt and Emory—the so-called Southern Ivies—or with the venerable University of Virginia, the Duke English department was not in that same league. Some Duke faculty members with stellar academic pedigrees—degrees from institutions like Brown, Penn, Harvard, Yale—privately felt that their careers were less than successes because they had ended up as faculty at a place like Duke rather than an institution more like where they had been trained. This sense that the department was second rate, together with the lack of a strong sense of community, had become over the years a kind of self-fulfilling prophecy. Stanley had a lot of work to do.

He began by hosting large parties—and many of them. He and Jane had bought a two-story ranch-style house nestled in the trees on Longwood Drive in the Stoneridge subdivision. Their next-door neighbor was the world famous theologian and intellectual Stanley Hauerwas.

With its sprawling lawn, the house was perfect for entertaining. He would invite not only the entire department, but also administrators, faculty from other departments, and even the English faculty from nearby University of North Carolina. It was not unusual for over three hundred guests to attend one of these gala events. His formula for a successful party was simple: order more food than you imagine your guests would ever be able to eat and invite more guests than you believe could possibly fit into the available space; everything else will take care of itself. In one end-of-year party, everyone of importance in the entire state seemed to be in attendance. The caterers had erected a huge tent on the lawn, and everything was perfect. Stanley emerged from inside his home dressed in a gleaming white suit. He stood for a while, Havana cigar in hand, watching the crowd, beaming with pleasure. It seemed to some a scene straight out of *The Great Gatsby*.

To strengthen the sense of community within the department, he instituted a series of regular colloquia. Fashioned loosely after the Tudor and Stuart Club at Hopkins but without the question-and-answer blood fest, these colloquia were opportunities for faculty to showcase their recent research to their colleagues and students. After a thorough search of the campus, he found the perfect venue: a room in the student union typically reserved for student events rather than for academic purposes. Despite initial objections he convinced the powers-that-be that his colloquia would greatly benefit students, since many graduate students would be in the audience. He then commanded everyone in the department to attend these events, and, to the surprise of many, most did attend. Early on he had sensed that some of the department's old guard feared being marginalized by the new regime, so he invited them to be among the first to give papers. They responded with surprise and gratitude. The colloquia soon generated an atmosphere of excitement in the department, and even the old guard began to feel that they were part of something important.

Stanley loved administrative work. As department chair at Hopkins, he learned to enjoy the challenges of organizational tasks, and management tasks in general. Most of all, he loved attempting to establish conditions that release the energies of scholars. He felt that academic bureaucracy is constructed in such a way as to repress the energy of scholars, so his goal as an administrator was to reverse that repression. One thing that he instinctually knew was the importance of the physical atmosphere of the workplace, so he went about improving the physical plan of the department in a number of ways. He was shocked to discover that English department faculty offices were scattered in many locations rather than being consolidated in one physical space—some offices were on one floor, some on another; some were in the administration building; others were in the library; and yet others were in the social sciences building. It's very hard to build community when everyone is scattered to the four winds, he thought to himself. The English department had half of one floor, and the other half was taken up by university accounting workers, who toiled in small cubicles. In fact, one had to walk through the accounting area in order to access the elevator. Stanley was walking through that area one day, and he suddenly realized the possibilities. He stopped, looked around, and in his booming voice announced, "I want this space!" Startled workers looked up from their spreadsheets, not exactly sure what he meant. He then went about persuading the administration that consolidating the English department would be an investment that would pay off. He convinced the dean and then the provost. To the surprise of many, central administration approved the plan. The accountants were moved out, and Stanley was given the opportunity to reconfigure the space. He arranged to bring all the faculty from the various outlying districts into the department, and he even got to choose all the color schemes—to the dismay of several of his colleagues, since he chose cool blue tones rather than earth tones as several of his colleagues urged.

What he found at Duke was a number of lifetime associate professors—scholars who had published enough scholarship to merit tenure and promotion to associate professor but whose career had then stalled. He investigated and discovered that several of these faculty members had long ago begun worthy scholarly projects but then had put them on the back burner. He blamed the stultifying climate of the department and its old-boy hierarchy for this state of affairs. He met individually with each one and made an agreement that he was certain he would be able to keep: "You complete this project, and I guarantee that I'll get you promoted to professor." This simple gesture was enough to energize most of these midcareer faculty, and Stanley followed through on his promise. He had remembered the wisdom of an old friend and colleague, the poet and critic Albert Cook, who had remarked, "Stanley, what would you rather have? A relatively undistinguished and unhappy associate professor, or a relatively undistinguished but happy full professor?" This wisdom seemed perfectly obvious to Stanley. You encourage someone whose career has stalled to produce *something*—which in effect announces to the world, "Hey, I'm still alive; the brain is still ticking"—and then you promote him. And this is exactly what he did.

Another initiative that contributed substantially to raising morale in the department was his effort to raise salary levels. He and Jane had been hired at very competitive salaries: his initial base salary before stipends for taking on administrative work was $100,000, which in 1985 was very respectable for a humanities professor. Jane's salary was in the $80,000s. He found the typical salaries in the department to be disgraceful. Some of these professors were productive scholars, yet they made close to nothing in his estimation. "Forget about merit pay," he said to Jane in frustration one hot and humid Friday evening: "These people haven't even been rewarded for being alive and breathing." So he set out to raise the salaries of faculty in the department incrementally. He was able to give larger than usual increases to many faculty, and over the span of his six years as chair, the department's overall salary base rose significantly.

While the colloquia and parties and salary increases and encouragement of associate professors all had very material effects, the real key to his storied success at Duke was his faculty recruitment efforts. He knew that the best way to build an academic department or college was to aggressively recruit top-notch faculty, especially senior scholars who were already considered to be among the best in the country. He also knew something that many in the academic world do not: you can maximize your success by recruiting dual-career couples who both are considered major scholars. As his own experience at Hopkins had taught him, faculties often have blinders on when it comes to making spousal accommodations. Not every partner is a so-called trailing spouse, a kind of dead weight that a department is asked to accept. Many prominent scholars have equally eminent partners, so hiring them both is a value-added bonus. What's more, once you hire a dual-career couple, you are likely to retain them, because finding two academic appointments elsewhere is difficult. Stanley would capitalize on the fact that many institutions fail to make this distinction between a trailing spouse and a dual-career power couple. Even before arriving at Duke, he fantasized about this strategy. "We'll create not only a welcoming attitude toward couples but an absolutely positive project of hiring them," he said to Jane late one evening, "especially couples where one of them had to commute or was in a situation where they were less than fully enfranchised academically." And then he joked, "When we're done, we'll have a university known as Couples U. Our motto will be 'Two for Two and All for Two,' and the school anthem will be 'Two for Tea.'"

He actively set out to recruit some of the most accomplished scholars in the nation, especially those in dual-career relationships. Over his six years as chair, he would hire an impressive cohort of major scholars— some in the English department, and some in the literature department, chaired by his friend and ally, Fredric Jameson. The famous Marxist critic Terry Eagleton came as a visiting professor for a year with his then-partner Toril Moi. After they broke up, Eagleton returned to Great Britain, and Moi accepted a permanent position at Duke. Moi herself was considered part of the international intellectual elite, and her *Sexual/ Textual Politics: Feminist Literary Theory*, which had come out in 1985, was considered a major contribution to scholarship. It would eventually be translated into eleven languages and in 2002 would be republished in a second edition—a rarity in scholarly publishing and a sure sign of the book's significance.

Stanley also recruited the medievalist Lee Patterson from Johns Hopkins and his wife Annabel Patterson, a Renaissance scholar at the University of Maryland. Realizing what a loss Annabel would be to the University of Maryland English department, the then-president William Kirwan attempted to persuade her to stay, but the lure of an appointment along with her husband in what was clearly going to become one of the best English departments in the nation was too strong.

Another major hire was Eve Kosofsky Sedgwick, a theorist of gender studies whose scholarship helped create the field of queer studies. Her *Between Men: English Literature and Male Homosocial Desire* had also come out in 1985 and was instantly considered a defining work of queer studies. Joining Sedgwick was another queer theorist, Michael Moon, and the Americanist and cultural studies scholar Janice Radway, whose *Reading the Romance* (1984) is considered a classic work of scholarship on popular culture. The neopragmatist literary theorist Barbara Herrnstein Smith also joined the faculty and would become a lifelong friend of Jane and Stanley's, as would the distinguished African American literature scholar Houston Baker.

Even the African American studies giant Henry Louis Gates Jr.—perhaps the only other English studies scholar with a reputation outside of the discipline to rival Stanley's—came for a year. Gates did not stay long at Duke, reportedly in part because the residual attitudes toward African Americans and Jews at Duke were barely hidden under the surface. Even some of the black faculty seemed to resent him because they had, in different ways, made their peace with Duke and its old-boy network. He would later refer to Duke as "The Plantation." Of course, it didn't help matters that the flamboyant scholar was rumored to have negotiated a staggeringly large salary and perks.

Certainly, there were other distinguished scholars hired in those years. Among them were David Aers, an expert in medieval literature and theology; Cathy Davidson, a specialist in the history and theory of technology; Karla FC Holloway, a scholar of African American cultural studies; and Jonathan Goldberg, a Renaissance literature specialist.

"Hello, Michael. Come to Duke. Let me make you rich! And I'll hire your wife, as well." Stanley was speaking to Michael Fried, the Princeton- and Harvard-trained modernist art critic and historian at Johns Hopkins. A brilliant scholar and a close friend and colleague of Stanley's, Fried, in the end, declined Stanley's generosity and persistence. He was thoroughly cathected to Hopkins despite the lure of largesse, but Stanley's aggressive salesmanship was more often successful than not with those he chose to pursue.

As word spread that Stanley was building a department of superstars at Duke, people across the country took notice. Professors not only in English departments but in many disciplines would discuss the latest news from Duke as if they were describing the latest episode of some television suspense serial. The national news media picked up on the story, further generating intense interest. Some called what was going on at Duke "crass entrepreneurialism," suggesting that it was unseemly for universities to attempt to buy themselves first-rate departments. More sympathetic observers saw it as entirely appropriate—after all, it works for sports teams; why not for academic departments?

Each year Stanley would host a Duke English department cocktail party at the annual Modern Language Association (MLA) convention, inviting hundreds of people. The Duke soirees immediately became one of the "must attend" receptions at the convention. Guests flooded into the party to mingle with the celebrity Duke crowd. Rather than pay the hotel's exorbitant prices for liquor—after all, he had no departmental budget to fund receptions—the enfant terrible and a staff member would purchase what he needed at a local discount store, usually Costco or Sam's Club, and then clandestinely smuggle it into his hotel suite, thereby breaking the hotel's rules. Hotel officials caught wind of the Duke party one year, when it became too raucous, and attempted to shut it down. Stanley deftly calmed the two agitated hotel officials down and quietly slipped them two crisp hundred-dollar bills. They walked away smiling.

As the reputation of the Duke English department skyrocketed, the quality of the graduate students increased dramatically and rapidly. Prospective graduate students from across the nation rushed to apply to the Duke program, hoping to have the opportunity to study with and perhaps become the protégé of this or that professor. The program saw an unprecedented surge in applications, and the department was in the enviable position of being able to become very selective in whom they admitted.

So, too, was there a noticeable boost in the department's collective pride and sense of self-worth. Suddenly, those who had felt that their careers were failures and who would slink around the MLA convention somewhat embarrassed that their name tags boldly announced that they were at Duke rather than Harvard, now proudly displayed them. Colleagues would approach them at the conference, glance at their tags, and excitedly say, "Oh, you're at Duke. What an exciting place! What's been going on there recently? Do you know so-and-so? Would you introduce me?" Perhaps being at Duke was not such a bad thing after all.

Of course, Duke was far from the first superstar English department, but what distinguished it from other powerhouse programs was that most—like those at Yale and Hopkins—grew methodically and organically over time, whereas the Duke department rose (and plummeted) in a relatively short period of time. Also, the historically notable departments tended to have strength over multiple disciplinary areas, whereas many (but not all) of the scholars that Stanley hired were in one way or another associated with the revolutionary new trends in critical theory: poststructuralism, African American studies, feminist theory, Marxist theory, queer theory.

Stanley had a particularly good year in 1989. He was appointed fellow of the Humanities Institute at the University of California at Irvine, joining such luminaries as Jacques Derrida, Geoffrey Hartman, and Wolfgang Iser. He would spend the spring semester at Irvine, and his assistant chair, Wallace Jackson, would cover his administrative duties at Duke. He and Jane rented a house in the hills of Laguna Beach. Stanley had finally found his personal paradise; it became his favorite place in the world. He quickly established the perfect routine. He would get up in the morning and run the five blocks down the hill and emerge in the center of town. He would stop at the basketball courts that were situated right on the beach and shoot hoops for a while with whoever happened to be there. Then he would run along the stunningly beautiful Pacific Coast Highway on the way back to the house. Meanwhile Jane would take the dog out for a romp on the beach, and then the couple would meet in a café overlooking the Pacific Ocean and have coffee and croissants. They then would walk back to the house, and he would get ready to go to the office. His only duties at the university were to participate in a formal three-hour meeting once a week and to be available for some time during the other weekdays, so he had a leisurely schedule. He would arrive at his office at about one thirty, stay for two hours, and make his way back to Laguna Beach, where he would meet Jane for a few sets of tennis. Then they would walk along the Pacific Coast Highway on the way to a restaurant for an early dinner. "Man, this is the way to live!" he said to Jane more than once.

That spring he rented his house in Chapel Hill to Henry Louis (Skip) Gates. Once in the middle of the semester Stanley had to return to North Carolina to attend to departmental business, and while there he decided to stop by his house. He parked in the driveway, and as he walked up the path, Gates came out onto the porch, looked with feigned sternness at Stanley, and asked, "May I help you?" as if Stanley were a trespasser on his own property. Stanley grinned, "That's vintage Skip Gates," he shouted. "Great to see you."

Also in 1989 Stanley received the Milton Society of America's James Holly Hanford Award for the most outstanding essay on Milton published that year for his "Spectacle and Evidence in *Samson Agonistes*," which was published in *Critical Inquiry*. And Duke University Press published his *Doing What Comes Naturally: Change, Rhetoric, and the Practice of Theory in Literary and Legal Studies*. Like many of his books, this one collected his most recent articles. The twenty-two essays in the book address a wide range of subjects from antiprofessionalism, the nature of rhetoric, and literary and legal interpretation, to antifoundationalism and, as always, Milton. With his academic utopia in mind, he dedicated this book to Kenneth Abraham, Michael Fried, Walter Michaels, and, tellingly, Baltimore, Maryland.

Two years later, in 1991, Stanley was named that year's Honored Scholar by the Milton Society of America, an annual award given for notable contributions to Milton scholarship. He also embarked on a national debate tour with conservative author Dinesh D'Souza. They would hold major debates at five institutions, including the University of Alabama, Northern Illinois University, and the University of South Florida. Both men were skilled debaters, and both knew how to entertain a crowd. D'Souza's debate style followed the method he developed in his books, especially *Illiberal Education*. He proceeded by amassing copious anecdotes, one after another, on the way to making a single point, each anecdote being riveting or shocking. Stanley, on the other hand, would mount sophisticated arguments based on data, evidence, and historical facts. While the debate series was generally considered a tie, many audience members responded favorably to D'Souza's glib and pithy anecdotes. Stanley's intellectual and sometimes even brilliant explanations were not nearly as entertaining as D'Souza's narratives, carefully honed by staff members at the conservative American Enterprise Institute. On the road, the two debaters became fast friends. They would play tennis and enjoy cocktails together. Two decades after the debates D'Souza would become the president of a small Christian college, King's College, until he resigned amid a scandal over an extramarital affair. He would continue to pay visits to Jane and Stanley in their home in Delray Beach when he happened to be in town for a fund-raising event.

When Stanley's five-year term as department chair reached an end in 1991, many colleagues encouraged him to sign on for another term. He refused. He felt that he had done all he could do. He was bored. Besides, he wanted to take on more advanced administrative posts, new challenges. He agreed to remain department chair for one additional year, through 1992. He always believed that a single five-year term was the perfect length of time to inhabit any administrative position: you spend the first year trying to figure out the lay of the land; once you know what is possible and what is not, you spend the second year formulating your plans for change; you spend the third year and fourth years implementing your plans; and the fifth year is for ensuring that everything got done as planned and is working well.

While it is true that his future administrative posts—as a press director and as a college dean—would both be five-year terms, this plan was more one in theory than in practice. It certainly was not the formula that he used in any of his administrative posts. Rather than methodically learn the lay of the land and spend substantial time formulating a plan, he always moved with lightning speed. One reason he was able to implement so many changes at Duke so quickly was that he met very little sustained resistance to his initiatives. He had learned early on that resistance to change is only successful if that resistance goes unchallenged, that those complaining about change depend on the agents of change falling back and fleeing in disarray in response to opposition. Whenever he heard that someone was unhappy with a proposed change, he would immediately sit down with that person and begin a dialogue about the relative merits of the change. He did not always win the person over, but this process effectively stunted any organized opposition to his initiatives.

Although Stanley is credited with creating one of the most stellar English departments in recent memory, it was not without its problems and controversies, and a sizable number of the original cohort he had recruited would eventually leave for other appointments. While morale during Stanley's term was greatly improved from what it had been when he first arrived, the department increasingly suffered from internal disputes and strife. Among academic disciplines, English departments are notoriously contentious. Part of this arises from the fact that the discipline of English studies encompasses such a wide variety of areas of study and diverse subdisciplines, and part arises from the fact that faculty in the discipline are trained to be agonistic, to ferret out weaknesses in an argument and to launch counterarguments. So an English department, especially one chock full of giant egos and prima donnas, as was the Duke department, always has the potential to be rife with cliques and turmoil. An old joke among provosts and deans goes something like this: If a dean's nightmare is an English department, what would hell be? The answer: *two* English departments. The Duke English department in the late 1980s proved to be more than a headache for many in the administration, including the university president.

Some of the conflict came from some of the faculty that Stanley had hired who felt, ironically, that he showed favoritism to the veteran members of the department. Some of the conflict arose from ideological struggles over the curriculum, which under Stanley was evolving to be rather loose and nontraditional. More traditional scholars, even among the new cohort, favored a more structured curriculum with requirements that ensured better coverage of a greater number of literary periods and figures. Another area of conflict involved what was perceived to be a clique of queer studies faculty. One of Stanley's star appointments was Eve Kosofsky Sedgwick, one of the founders of queer studies. She was, if not herself cliquish, a figure around whom people orbited in a way that constituted a clique and seemed to present an unwelcoming face to those on the outside. This circle included several faculty and graduate students. Whether it was a fair assessment or not, many in the department felt that the group was exclusionary, and this perception created substantial tension. Some members of the group felt that the real problem was not their cliquishness but homophobia and the inability to perceive the value of their work. Various confrontations between members of this group and other department members led to unpleasantness, harsh words, sore feelings, and resentments. Many department members found themselves embroiled in these battles.

Compounding the growing internal ferment was the fact that the department became the center of the so-called culture wars nationally. During the 1980s, the political right wing in the United States had declared war on what they perceived to be the subversion of traditional Western values by left-leaning intellectuals and artists. They believed (and still do) that university professors in particular were responsible for indoctrinating students into becoming Marxists, atheists, relativists, and supporters of abortion rights and gay and other alternative lifestyles. The rapid growth of feminism seemed to threaten the structure of the core American institution—the family—while affirmative action and multiculturalism seemed to threaten the very fabric of society, what it meant to be an American. The epicenter of this war was school and university curricula. Conservatives knew that if they were to be successful in halting the progress of these movements, they would need to prevent teachers from controlling the curriculum.

Conservative commentators decried the fact that in some colleges, students might be able to have graduated having read works by Toni

Morrison or J. R. R. Tolkien or Ray Bradbury but not Chaucer or Shake-speare or Milton. They perceived the new focus on global cultures as a way to teach students that Western civilization was not superior to other cultures. They especially hated the fact that practically no one in the academy took creationism seriously. It was the height of the Reagan years, and the cry was that tenured radicals were destroying American culture. Prominent conservative cultural warriors included Reagan's secretary of education, William Bennett; the author and chair of the National Endowment for the Humanities (and wife of the future vice president), Lynne Cheney; and writer and Reagan advisor (and author of *Illiberal Education*), Dinesh D'Souza. These and other conservative pundits engaged in a relentless attack on higher education, arguing that it had lost its bearing in its attempts to be "politically correct."

In June of 1987 a conservative Slavic languages professor at Duke, Magnus Krynski, gave a speech at a meeting of Accuracy in Academia in Washington, D.C., in which he condemned the Duke English de-partment for amassing a department full of "Marxist celebrities" such as Stanley and Jane. A Raleigh newspaper reported on the speech and interviewed Stanley, who stated that while he certainly was no Marxist, he did not believe it would have been such a horrible thing if he were. This statement enraged Hoover Adams, the founding editor and pub-lisher of an independent, family-owned newspaper in North Carolina called the *Daily Record*. Hoover was a member of the state's conservative elite and a friend of archconservative Senator Jesse Helms. He began a prolonged letter-writing campaign to attempt to force Stanley and the Duke administration to either confirm or deny that they approved of having "communists" on the faculty of such a prominent "Christian-supported" university as Duke. He began by writing Stanley in October of 1987 asking for clarification. In his letter he pointed out that Fredric Jameson had been quoted as saying that he believed that his duty as a professor was to do everything he could to foster a Marxist culture in the nation. When Stanley did not reply, Adams continued to send letters, not only to him but to Jameson and to Duke's president, H. Keith Brodie.

It fell to the provost, Phillip Griffiths, to respond on behalf of the president. He gave the usual response: universities are committed to fostering free expression of ideas, and it would be inappropriate to at-tempt to suppress them. Nonetheless, the provost invited Hoover to visit Duke and perhaps even interview Stanley and Jameson. Hoover declined, saying that he doubted the professors would talk to him even if he were to visit, yet he continued his letter-writing campaign, sending additional letters to the provost and other university officials. Conservative commentators used the Duke English department as well as Stanford University, which had recently modernized its general education curriculum to be more culturally diverse and sensitive, as examples of what was wrong with higher education. They argued in major newspapers across the nation and abroad that left-wing radicals had seized control of the nation's elite institutions of higher learning and were training students to become future revolutionaries. The furor reached a fever pitch on November 13, 1990, when the Rush Limbaugh Show aired a segment excoriating the Duke University administration for allowing un-American activities to go on under their very noses and probably with their consent, and Dorothy Rabinowitz published a column, "Vive the Academic Resistance," in the *Wall Street Journal* suggesting that students at Duke were being brainwashed. In an effort to quell the uproar, President Brodie published a letter to the editor in the *Wall Street Journal*, reassuring the public that scholarly debate from all perspectives was alive and well at his institution. As evidence he pointed to the lively debate over the possible formation of a Duke chapter of the National Association of Scholars (NAS), an organization of conservative professors opposed to "the rising threat of politicization of colleges and universities." This lively debate might more accurately be described as a firestorm, and one that Stanley was smack in the middle of.

The National Association of Scholars had been founded three years earlier, in 1987, and it promptly set out to form affiliate chapters in colleges across the nation. Incensed by what he perceived to be the radicalization of the Duke English department and the deterioration of the curriculum, a Duke political science professor, James Barber, quietly sent a letter to colleagues he believed to be like-minded informing them that he was organizing a campus affiliate of NAS and inviting them to become founding members. The letter contained a list of twenty-six Duke faculty members, fifteen of them chaired professors, who had already signed on to be listed as founding members. The group included two English professors, part of the old guard. Barber's plan was to quietly enlist as many founding members as possible before issuing a general invitation to the entire Duke community. Colleagues who received this "confidential" letter but who were not sympathetic sent copies to Stanley. He immediately published a letter to the editor in the student-run newspaper, the *Chronicle*, informing the campus about the "clandestine" effort to form a Duke chapter of NAS and pointing out that the organization was widely known to be racist, sexist, and homophobic. Believing that liberals in any ideological battle always make the tactical error of attempting to be too "fair" and "nice," thereby assuring that they will lose, he then took a page from the conservative playbook and chose to be proactive: he fired off a letter to the provost suggesting that perhaps anyone who signed up to be a member of a racist, sexist, and homophobic organization such as NAS should not be appointed to key academic committees such as those dealing with academic standards and promotion and tenure. This action itself proved to be a tactical error. His letter was somehow made public, touching off a conflagration that polarized many on the campus and across the nation.

While many agreed that NAS represented a kind of thought police intent on imposing its conservative viewpoints on others, many people both on and off campus were outraged by Stanley's recommendation, saying it constituted the very kind of censorship that he was attempting to prevent. He was forced to clarify his position in another letter to the provost and to the local press. He reaffirmed that he believed NAS to be a sexist, racist, and homophobic organization but said that he did not literally mean that its members should be banned from university committees, just that he expected all committee members to approach their work with intellectual integrity, not from preconceived political positions. The provost made clear to the campus that there would be no a priori litmus test in making committee appointments.

Another group of faculty began circulating a petition against NAS, calling it hostile to curricular change that was more inclusive of women and minorities. They published a full-page ad in the *Chronicle* calling NAS's stance on multiculturalism "regrettable" and applauding all efforts to strengthen diversity in the curriculum. It was signed by ninety-three faculty members, including Stanley, Henry Louis Gates, Fred Jameson, Toril Moi, Janice Radway, and Eve Sedgwick. The Executive Committee of the Academic Council, the primary faculty governance organ of the university, felt compelled to issue a statement concerning the controversy.

The committee said that it would not take a side in the controversy, but it reaffirmed that the faculty at Duke had a strong commitment to increasing diversity on campus; it urged both sides to engage in civil debate. Prior to issuing this statement, President Brodie had addressed the group, assuring them that Duke was firmly committed to academic freedom and would never censure anyone for expressing their beliefs. In the pages of the local press, he promised the community that Duke will always protect free inquiry and expression.

Faculty on both sides of the issue published countless letters to the editor in Duke's *Chronicle*, calling each other intolerant and anti-intellectual. Some pointed out that NAS was funded in part by the right-wing John M. Olin and Sarah Scaife Foundations. One even likened the organization to a latter-day Ku Klux Klan. The *Chronicle* ran numerous articles on the feud, as did the professional newspapers in the state, and soon the story was being reported on by the national press. One article in the *National Review* referred to the "epistemological fascism" at Duke. Both Stanley and President Brodie were then deluged with angry letters not only from across the nation but internationally. Some defended NAS as an organization; others demanded an explanation of how NAS is racist and sexist; still others expressed outrage that Stanley would dare recommend that NAS membership be the basis for not appointing faculty to important committees. For the most part both Stanley and the president took these letters seriously, responding in lengthy, reasoned, and polite letters. Of course, not all of the letters Stanley received on this issue were critical or hostile. Many commended him for taking a courageous stand against NAS. Then, on November 27, the *Chronicle* published an open letter to the Duke community, inviting anyone who believed in rational discourse and a free and democratic society to apply for membership to NAS. It listed forty-six Duke professors as founding members. Many were chaired professors.

Another controversy that raged simultaneously with the battles with NAS involved Holocaust denial. On November 5, 1991, the *Chronicle* published an "advertisement" that insisted that the Holocaust had never really happened, paid for by a neo-Nazi group, the Committee for Open Debate on the Holocaust, which was headed by Bradley R. Smith. The ad was actually an exposition meant to persuade readers that the Holocaust was a conspiracy perpetrated by the Jews. This racist tract shocked and angered practically the entire campus. Many called for shutting down the newspaper and for punishing the editors. President Brodie and his advisors scrambled to determine what their official response should be. He consulted with Stanley, among others, about his response and eventually concluded that taking punitive action would potentially violate the First Amendment but that he should issue a strong statement to the campus. He said in a statement released the next day that he deplored the effort to conceal the truth about the Holocaust and that as a community of scholars Duke was committed to seeking the truth at all times. He explained that while it was tempting to take action against the newspaper, Duke also had a strong commitment to the First Amendment. He hoped that the university community would use this event as an occasion to refamiliarize itself with the real facts concerning the Holocaust. Stanley wrote to Brodie saying that he agreed that punitive action would have been inappropriate but that he was very troubled by the fact that the president failed to sharply criticize the newspaper's action.

The furor on campus seemed to intensify by the hour. Some faculty wrote letters to the newspaper in protest. Others organized a protest rally. Still others held a panel discussion on the First Amendment. The history department published in the *Chronicle* a full-page rebuttal of the neo-Nazi tract, outlining the real facts about the Holocaust. It was signed and paid for by the entire faculty of the department. Two members of the newspaper's editorial board resigned over the controversy. Some faculty attempted to circulate a petition condemning the publication of the treatise, but it stalled. A professor in the religion department, Kalman Bland, sent a long letter to the faculty newsletter chastising Duke faculty and administrators for their silence and for not joining the history faculty in publicly speaking out. The controversy simmered awhile and eventually died down, but it inspired Stanley to write a number of works about the limits of the First Amendment and about Holocaust denial.

He included some of his works on these subjects in his next book, *There's No Such Thing as Free Speech, and It's a Good Thing, Too*, published by Oxford University Press in 1994. The book contains eighteen essays on such subjects as reverse racism, liberalism, interdisciplinarity, legal interpretation, and Milton studies. In the title essay he addresses the types of issues being debated over the Holocaust denial controversy at Duke. He argues that as a concept "free speech" falls apart under scrutiny. "Free speech" is the label we confer on speech that furthers agendas or supports values we are in favor of; speech that threatens those agendas or values is a candidate for regulation or restriction. In fact, it is the very restriction (what would be wrong to utter) that makes possible its positive alternative. Free speech, then, is not some general principle or value in and of itself; it is always tied to some political, practical value at play in the real world. Once we understand that there is no genuinely "free" speech—that is, no language unaffected by ideology—then perhaps we won't be so squeamish about restricting certain language such as hate speech. He uses the story of the neo-Nazi propaganda at Duke as an example. The student editor knew that the treatise was racist and personally disagreed with it, yet she felt compelled to publish it. Had she not fallen prey to the usual misunderstanding of free speech as some pure phenomenon that exists in and of itself, she might have felt empowered to reject the tract in the first place. The book went on to win a national award: the PEN/Spielvogel-Diamonstein Award for a collection of essays that "exemplifies the dignity and esteem of the essay form."

In 1993 Jane and Stanley would move to another house: a beautiful, architect-designed lakefront home. Jane had been away at a spiritual retreat for nine days, and Stanley was at loose ends—as he always was when she was away. He never could quite understand her interest in Eastern philosophies; it just seemed too reminiscent of the 1960s to him. He had just finished playing basketball at the gym that Saturday, and he wandered into a nearby café for a cup of coffee. Stanley is the type who cannot simply sit still; he must read something while drinking his coffee. The shop had no newspapers, so he idly picked up a real estate flyer and began to study it. He noticed a house for sale on a lake in Chapel Hill that the locals colloquially referred to as Grandmother's Lake. One of their colleagues in the French department had a house in that area, across the street from the lake, and Jane had been fascinated by the thought of living on the lake. Stanley took another sip of coffee and thought to himself, "Well, I haven't got anything to do, so I'll go take a look at it." He drove to the neighborhood and discovered that the realtor was sponsoring an open house, so he took a tour. Disappointed, he found the house unacceptable. As he drove around the lake he noticed a for-sale sign posted on the lawn of a very attractive house nestled in the trees and right on the lake. It was gorgeous. He dialed the realtor's number listed on the sign, and the eager agent promised to meet him there immediately. The house was perfect. As it turned out, it was in a short-sale situation; the restaurateur who owned it had gone bankrupt. They agreed on the spot on a good price: $234,000. Later that evening Stanley was to pick Jane up from the airport. They embraced, got into the car, and Stanley said, "I want to show you something before we go home." He drove her to the house, and they strolled around the property and sat on the deck looking at the shimmering lake and watching with fascination the copious ducks, Kingfishers, and Great Blue Herons. Jane loved the house and the property. Stanley had already made an appointment with the realtor for the next morning. They met with the realtor at eleven o'clock that Sunday and bought the house.

Also that year, 1993, they bought a second home in the village of Andes in New York, about three and a half hours from New York City in the western Catskills. This spectacular vacation home rests on a small mountain, overlooking a reservoir and five mountain peaks on the other side of the reservoir. No homes or other signs of civilization clutter their view of the breathtakingly beautiful landscape. The house is on a forty-acre parcel of land and has a rustic, raw-wood aesthetic. The ground-floor great room itself is twelve hundred square feet with a soaring vaulted ceiling over twenty feet high, and both Jane and Stanley have spacious studios. Every year for decades they would spend much of their summer here in the quiet and secluded Shangri-la.

After Stanley completed his six years as chair, he was enjoying his freedom from the daily headaches of chairing an academic department. It was 1993, and he had traveled to Hollywood to attend a conference on the television series *The Fugitive*, a subject he would eventually write a book on. He was relaxing in his hotel room, which had a good view of the famed Grauman's Chinese Theatre across the street, when the telephone rang. On the other end was Duke's then provost Thomas Langford and Steven Cohn, the journals manager of Duke University Press. To his surprise, the provost opened the discussion by saying, "Stanley, I want you to become executive director of the press. We'll also give you the title of associate provost. What do you think?" Stanley was already associated with the press. Both he and Fred Jameson were serving as members of the press's editorial board, and they both had attempted to support the press by establishing a book series and encouraging colleagues around the nation to publish their books in it. Called Post-Contemporary Interventions, the series focused on critical theory in a wide range of disciplinary areas. They both recently published their own books in the series: Stanley's *Doing What Comes Naturally: Change, Rhetoric, and the Practice of Theory in Literary and Legal Studies* had come out in 1989, and Jameson's masterpiece *Postmodernism: The Cultural Logic of Late Capitalism* was released in 1991. They discussed the directorship for a while, and Stanley promised to consider it.

By the time he returned to Durham three days later, he had decided that directing the press might be interesting and challenging work. He consulted with Jane, and they both thought that this would be a good career move. He finally decided to accept the position, but then a problem arose: word had leaked out that he might become director of the press, and several conservative faculty were up in arms. They shouted that he would ruin the press just as he had, in their estimation, ruined the English department. Duke's new president, Nannerl "Nan" Keohane, began to back away from the decision to appoint Stanley. The last thing she needed as a new president was controversy. She called Stanley to her office and told him about the resistance to his appointment and said she was not yet sure what she wanted to do. She offered to revisit the decision after things quieted down a bit. Stunned, Stanley said firmly, "Look, Nan, if you wait for things to quiet down before you do anything, you'll never do anything." He was furious. The president said that she would think about it, and they agreed to talk in a week or two. When they next met, she said that she had thought it over and that she did want to appoint him executive director after all. The press needed his leadership.

What Stanley did not know was the extent to which the press was in crisis. The university's central administration believed that the leadership of the press was withholding vital data from them about its poor fiscal health. The press had far exceeded its budget that year, and no one had warned the administration. Like many university presses in those days, Duke University Press was in severe financial debt and relied on the university to bail it out. The administration had demanded a rescue plan from the previous director and was dissatisfied with his plan. The director was subsequently fired, and there was serious talk of closing the press down permanently. Many universities across the country were reducing their subsidies to their university presses and were demanding that they move toward self-sustainability. This is exactly what the Duke administration hoped for. Stanley was a logical choice to turn the press around given his international reputation and his experience building Duke's English department.

Stanley approached his new job as he did everything: with speed and enthusiasm. His goal was to duplicate and even surpass the success of the University of Minnesota Press, which had cultivated a reputation for publishing avant-garde, cutting-edge theoretical works. He devised a two-pronged strategy: he would draw on his friendships to encourage several nationally prominent senior scholars to publish their next books with the press, and he would actively solicit first-book manuscripts from junior scholars who seemed destined themselves to become nationally prominent. The strategy worked. He was able to convince Walter Benn Michaels to publish his *Our America: Nativism, Modernism, and Pluralism*; Annette Kolodny to publish her *Failing the Future: A Dean Looks at Higher Education in the Twenty-First Century*; and Darryl Gless and Barbara Herrnstein Smith to publish *The Politics of Liberal Education*, a collection of works by some of the most prominent scholars in the nation, including Mary Louise Pratt, Richard Lanham, Gerald Graff, Henry Louis Gates, Henry Giroux, Eve Kosofsky Sedgwick, and Richard Rorty. These works along with his own and Jameson's books gave instant notoriety to the press. In the eyes of many, by 1998, when he stepped down as executive director, Stanley had certainly achieved his goal of rivaling if not surpassing the University of Minnesota Press. In later life, he would say that directing the press was the best job he had ever had. He loved the combination of intellectual and business concerns. All decisions had to be made against the background of two concerns: the elevation of the quality of books being published balanced against the financial constraints on the press. The subsidy that the press received from the university was in a period of planned decline. The press was going to have to become self-sustaining. So the intellectual concerns of publishing cutting-edge scholarship always had to be made with the bottom line in mind.

At one point early in Stanley's tenure as director, it looked like the press was going to have another bad year, fiscally. The press could ill afford another fiscal crisis, since the administration was seriously considering terminating it altogether. The journal's editor, Steve Cohn, made a proposal to Stanley. In the 1990s, several commercial publishers were attempting to acquire scholarly journals, especially those with high prestige and large circulations. Cohn proposed that the press sell one of its longstanding scholarly periodicals, the *Journal of Personality*. This proved to be a wise business decision. The journal was ready to expand, but the press was cash-strapped and was not publishing books in the discipline of psychology. Stanley agreed to sell the journal to the highest bidder, and the press announced an auction. Wiley-Blackwell ended up purchasing the journal for a substantial amount of money, which not only allowed the press to survive what otherwise would have been another year deep in the red, but it allowed Stanley and his staff to make investments toward the next several years.

Midway through his tenure as press director, in 1995, Stanley would spend the spring semester serving as distinguished visiting faculty fellow at the Center for Ideas and Society at the University of California at Riverside. He would still fulfill his duties as director, flying home when needed. His main duty at Riverside was to lead a seminar for faculty members focusing on various issues of interpretation and critical theory. Early in January, he, Jane, and their dog made the journey across the continent in their red convertible Jaguar. He had flown out to the area the month before and, working with a realtor, had narrowed the housing options down to two: a small bungalow near the university in Riverside, and a lakeside lodge forty-five minutes away in the resort community of Bear Mountain. The Riverside home was convenient but dreary; the Bear Mountain residence was stunning, but he had been warned that sudden winter storms were frequent and could trap residents in the mountain town for days.

When they arrived at the Riverside home, Jane took one look at the low-slung California-style house, turned to Stanley, and said, "You have got to be kidding! This is dreadfully dreary." Always sensitive to Jane's desires, he answered, "Okay, tomorrow morning we'll go look at the Bear Mountain place." With their dog in the back seat, they left early the next morning. There should be plenty of time to get back to the airport by one thirty to pick up their cat, which was being shipped from North Carolina. Halfway to their destination they ran into a heavy snowstorm. Luckily, a street vendor was selling tire chains, so they stopped and had them installed for the long trip up the mountain road.

Although he had only been to the house once, he found it easily. They trudged down the sixty-two snow-covered steps leading from the street to the front door of the lakefront residence. Always good with numbers, Stanley remembered the code to unlock the realtor's lockbox, so they entered the home and took a tour. It was a beautiful lodge on a lovely lake.

In order to make their way back down the mountain to Riverside, they first needed to make it up the opposite side of the mountain. As they began their ascent in the blinding snow, the chains snapped. They were stuck. There was no way to drive up to the crest of the hill. They began knocking on doors in search of someone to help them, but many of the homes at that time of year were uninhabited because they were seasonal residences. Finally, a woman and her grown daughter took them in, and after a few hours they were able to find someone to tow them up the incline so they could make their way back down the mountain to Riverside. Their Riverside host, the philosopher Bernd Magnus, would rescue their cat from the airport. After their mountain ordeal, they decided to stay in the ugly home in Riverside. "That's it, Stanley," Jane said emphatically. "No more visiting professorships!"

Later that same year, 1995, Oxford University Press published Stanley's *Professional Correctness: Literary Studies and Political Change.* Two years earlier, he had delivered four lectures as part of the prestigious Clarendon Lectures series at Oxford, and the book was a publication of those lectures. His experience at Oxford had been quite pleasurable. The lectures were spread over a two-week period in the spring of 1993. It was exceedingly difficult to convince Jane to travel with him anywhere. He had to practically beg her to spend a week in Great Britain with him. Fortuitously, her cousin, a philosopher and scholar of Plato, was planning to visit Oxford at that same time and offered to take Jane's mother. So Jane relented and said she would come for the second week of Stanley's talks. When he first arrived at Oxford, an escort from Oxford University Press showed him what would be their suite of rooms in Christ College. He quickly scanned the rooms and was immediately disappointed: they were both too big and too small at the same time: cavernous in the wrong places, small and cramped in the wrong places. The furniture seemed to be vintage graduate student apartment furnishings. His escort observed the look of dismay on Stanley's face and was quick to reassure him: "These are well-thought-of quarters," she said. "Margaret Atwood has stayed here, and so has Stephen Greenblatt." Mischievous as ever, Stanley looked at her and replied sardonically, "Together?" She blushed.

"Look," he continued. "It is extraordinarily difficult for me to persuade my wife to join me on an occasion like this one. I was able to persuade her to come next week. The last thing I want is for her to walk into an accommodation that she will immediately dislike. We simply have to find something else." Eager to accommodate, the press representative helped him find a very comfortable suite of rooms in a nearby pub hotel overlooking a quaint courtyard. Stanley knew that Jane would love it. And she did. She fell in love with it instantly.

Even before they began, the lectures generated substantial excitement—the controversial academic celebrity from the States was certain to say something scandalous, and everyone wanted to be in attendance when it happened. The room was packed with onlookers. Some estimated that about six hundred people attended each of the four lectures. The Marxist critic Terry Eagleton was in attendance, as was the scholar and novelist David Lodge, the author of several popular novels about academic life in which Stanley is a thinly veiled character: Morris Zapp. So was Jane, her cousin, and her mother. Jane's mother beamed; she loved being in the aura of celebrity, and it was a special treat to be at one of the world's oldest and greatest universities. On off days, Stanley and Jane's family members were able to take in the sights, and they even sat "high table," a long tradition at Oxford and Cambridge Universities in which the dining hall was arranged so that undergraduates sat at long tables stretching the length of the hall, while the master, professors, and distinguished guests sat at a raised table at the head of the room perpendicular to the student tables.

Earlier that year Stanley had been nominated to become the next president of the State University of New York (SUNY) at Purchase, the arts-oriented campus in the SUNY system. The current president, Sheldon Grebstein, was retiring as leader of the institution of roughly four thousand students. Stanley's candidacy had progressed over time and a number of interviews. In the end, there were only two candidates: Stanley and Bill Lacy, the former president of Cooper Union in New York City. It was widely assumed by everyone that Stanley would be offered the position. He and Jane had had a triumphal visit to campus, where they had been shown the presidential residence and held discussions about how it might be renovated for them. The search committee—composed of representatives from the faculty, staff, students, alumni, and governing board—voted nine to two in Stanley's favor, with the board members abstaining, since the full board would eventually have to make the final decision. The governing board, constituted by gubernatorial appointment, was the body with the legal authority and responsibility to appoint a new president, and the board chose Lacy instead. A board member called Stanley during his first week in Great Britain to inform him. While Stanley was certainly disappointed, he was too preoccupied with preparing his lectures to think much about the presidential search, so he promptly forgot the bad news, neglecting to inform Jane in the process.

The decision to hire Lacy despite overwhelming support for Stanley ignited intense anger on campus. Committee members sent a strongly worded letter complaining about the board's action to D. Bruce Johnstone, the SUNY system chancellor, who in turn replied with an equally caustic letter demanding an apology for the offensive tone of their letter. The *New York Times* reported on the controversy in a June 13 article entitled "Behind SUNY's Choice for New President." Back in Durham, Jane was leisurely reading the newspaper that morning when she came across the article. She was furious. Red-faced, she telephoned the search committee chair, who was one of the trustees, and lambasted him. She had been an integral part of the process, yet no one from the committee had bothered to call her personally. She had had to learn the news from the newspapers. She was still seething when she joined Stanley in Oxford.

The lectures and the book that chronicles them were a great success but, like so many works that Stanley has published, very controversial. The main thesis of the lectures is that despite the claims of those who are attempting to transform literary studies so that the field is more directly connected with contemporary political issues—sexism, racism, homophobia, and so on—when literary critics are operating *as* academics within the constraints and forums of the discipline, they will necessarily be reaching only a relatively small number of people (their colleagues in the discipline) and thus will have little or no political effectiveness. Conversely, if they depart from the usual modes of expression, methodologies, and forums of the discipline and thereby discover some degree of political effectiveness outside of the academy, they will no longer be operating as literary critics: they will be operating as something *other* than literary critics. We may very well judge this new way of operating to be valuable—in fact, we may even value it more than we value a work of criticism—but the fact remains that such political work is *not* literary criticism; it is something different. What's more, this new work is not in and of itself superior or inferior to a work of criticism; it is, again, simply different.

This position enraged many in literary studies because throughout the 1970s and 1980s and still to this day, humanities professors have been increasingly introducing such political concerns into their pedagogy and scholarship. Many believed that finally they had made literary studies more relevant to contemporary life. To them, Stanley's position seemed to be a conservative, even right-wing, perspective. He seemed to be threatening the very way they had been conducting themselves as intellectuals. What they missed, however, was that he was not advocating that they stop introducing the political into their classrooms or scholarship; he was simply pointing out that they were fooling themselves if they believed that they were doing literary criticism when they were engaging in political advocacy. He would later expand on this theme in *Save the World on Your Own Time* (2008).

Another controversy that occurred while Stanley served as executive director of Duke University Press has been dubbed the Sokal Affair. In 1996 a New York University physics professor, Alan Sokal, published an article entitled "Transgressing the Boundaries: Towards a Transformative Hermeneutics of Quantum Gravity" in the Spring/Summer issue of *Social Text*, an interdisciplinary scholarly journal publishing work in cultural and critical theory. As soon as the article appeared in print, *Lingua Franca*, the academic world's answer to *People* magazine, published an exposé entitled "A Physicist Experiments with Cultural Studies" revealing that the *Social Text* article was in fact a hoax meant to reveal that postmodern scholarship in the humanities and social sciences was not intellectually rigorous, especially when that scholarship sets out to describe science as a "social construction." Sokal wrote the article in such a way that anyone well versed in science would immediately recognize it as a spoof, yet the journal editors—*Social Text* is edited by a "collective" of scholars who together make editorial decisions—assumed that a prominent physicist knew what he was talking about when it came to his own discipline and so took him at his word and published the work. The hoax immediately caused an uproar, with those supportive of postmodernist scholarship claiming that what Sokal had done constituted research misconduct, and those supportive of Sokal arguing that what he had done was a service to the academic world because it illustrated how easy it was to publish "nonsense" in some journals. Stanley was unfairly tarnished by the scandal. Many assumed that he had played a role in publishing Sokal's spoof because Duke University Press published and distributed *Social Text* and because his good friend Fred Jameson was one of the journal's founding editors. The fact is that *Social Text* was an independent journal that had a purely business relationship with the press. Stanley had no relationship with its editorial practices and values and, in fact, was philosophically opposed to editorial "collectives." Contributing to the misunderstanding was the fact that the *New York Times* urged him to write an op-ed piece about the affair, which he did, though reluctantly: "Professor Sokal's Bad Joke." His column generated hundreds of letters on both sides of the issue. So, for good or ill, Stanley's name has always been associated with the Sokal Affair.

In 1997 Harvard University Press published the second edition of *Surprised by Sin: The Reader in "Paradise Lost"* to mark the thirtieth anniversary of the original publication of the groundbreaking book. The book had been so successful that the press wisely judged that a new edition with an updated preface would be of interest to many readers. It would go on to win the Milton Society of America's James Holly Hanford Book Award for the most distinguished book on Milton in 1997. When he first received his advance copy of the book in the mail, he thumbed through it for a few minutes and then sat back in his chair and reminisced. He remembered back in 1966 when Adrienne and he were in London and he was working on the manuscript of *Surprised by Sin*. She was typing one of his pages, and he was proofreading another. He stopped, looked at her and said, "Adrienne, this book will make me famous." And it had.

In the mid-1990s Stanley was nominated for nearly twenty administrative posts across the country, many of which he became a semifinalist for but did not get the final offer. He was a candidate for president of Macalester College, a private liberal arts college in Saint Paul, Minnesota; provost at the University of California at Santa Barbara; and dean at the University of Kansas, the University of Georgia, Vanderbilt, and UCLA, among others. He progressed to the final three for dean of arts and sciences at Emory University and had scheduled campus interviews but had to cancel them when he came down with a bad case of influenza. During his time convalescing, he reflected on the job and decided that it was not a good fit for him. Besides, he thought to himself, half in jest, he hated the furniture in the dean's office. He withdrew from consideration.

On many of his interviews he repeatedly encountered a frustrating phenomenon: search committee members would intersperse questions about his intellectual views in with questions about his administrative skills and experience. They would want to know if he believed in objective truth, or whether he was a relativist, or whether he believed in the scientific method. He usually politely answered these questions, but finally at one interview he blurted out, "Those are totally different realms. There is no relationship between the answers that you give to certain questions in interpretive theory and the way in which you will engage in certain practical skills as an administrator." Apparently, the committee disagreed. Some committees were intimidated both by Stanley in person—after all, he is a very forceful personality—and by the extent of his academic résumé; most who compared their own list of accomplishments with his came up lacking. Despite these frustrations, he did make it a point to enjoy himself at each interview. At one interview, he was being given a tour of the campus, and he and his escort took a shortcut through the gym. They walked across the basketball court, and Stanley picked up a basketball at about half-court and to his escort's astonishment, sank it. The boy from the streets of Providence was alive and well.

When the University of Illinois at Chicago (UIC) began searching for a new dean of the College of Arts and Sciences in 1998, someone formally nominated Stanley. Elizabeth "Betsy" Hoffman was the provost at the time and was especially interested in putting the institution on the map. For too long this urban campus had had to suffer being the poor stepsister to the Urbana campus. The search committee forwarded the names of five finalists to the provost to interview, including Stanley's. She knew that Stanley could be just the person to help raise UIC's status, but given his reputation in the academic world, she was very skeptical that in the end he would come to Chicago or that he would be the right fit. She agreed to interview him along with the other four candidates, a few of whom she knew very well.

On his first night on campus Stanley was to have dinner with the provost, who had arranged to pick him up at his hotel. She arrived at the prescribed time with her husband, Brian, an adjunct professor of economics. Like Stanley, he was a car aficionado, and he had a collection of interesting cars. They arrived in a gorgeous 1993 BMW 850. On the way to the hotel, she had wondered why her husband had chosen a sports car to pick a candidate up in; it had virtually no backseat and very little leg room. Perhaps her husband knew that she was not so sure she wanted to hire Stanley and this was his private test of the candidate. Stanley strode out of the hotel door, up to the car, and exclaimed, "Wow! What a cool car! Will I get to ride in this car?" Her husband was instantly won over. Stanley climbed into the back seat, oohing and ahing over the sleek BMW. The provost was stunned. She had imagined a nerdy English professor who did work on weird rhetorical subjects. Within one minute Stanley had deflated her stereotype.

At the restaurant they engaged in a spirited conversation, first about cars, then about basketball—a passion all three shared. Both Betsy and Brian were tall and had played basketball in high school, though neither was tall enough to play college ball. By the time dinner was over, the three had bonded completely. The next day Stanley went on to win over the entire college. What became clear to many during Stanley's campus interview was that everything you thought you knew about him was untrue: far from being some wild-eyed radical, he was a thoughtful, almost middle-of-the-road academic entrepreneur who appreciated quality and was prepared to make tough decisions. What's more, he was fun to be with. He may have a reputation as an enfant terrible—occasionally deserved—but those who came to know him saw a smart, witty, entertaining professional.

After Stanley left for home, the challenge for the provost became the uncertainty: Will he really want this job or not? As it turned out, Stanley had fallen in love with UIC. He had made up his mind that he wanted to come to UIC and help raise its profile. He and the provost had agreed on a salary, but he was not going to accept an offer if Jane wasn't going to come too. It became clear that now the institution would need to woo Jane. It was up to Brian to recruit Jane. He spoke with her several times on the phone, and the university brought her to Chicago and gave her the royal treatment.

Ida (Weinberg) Fish at her wedding, April 7, 1932

Stanley Fish at five
years old with his two-
year-old sister, Rita

Stanley (standing by bookcase) and the senior high school yearbook
staff, 1955

Rita Fish, 1959

Ron Fish, high school
graduation photo, 1963

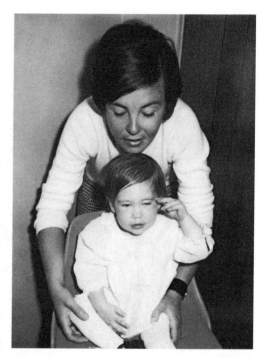

Adrienne (Aaron) Fish
with her daughter, Susan,
Berkeley, California, 1968

Stanley, 1975

Stanley and his daughter, Susan, at the Grand Canyon, circa 1975

Stanley and Jane Tompkins at wedding of John and Laura
Irwin, 1978

Jane's parents, Henry and Lucille Perry, 1979

Ida and Jane, 1980

Stanley and Jane at Club Med in the Bahamas, 1980

Ida, 1982

Stanley and Jane's wedding,
August 7, 1982

Stanley outside his Baltimore home, 1984

Jane, Durham, North Carolina, 1985

Photograph of Max
Fish taken by Stanley
(and later turned
into a painting),
Pompano Beach,
Florida, circa 1985

Max and Ida, 1987

Stanley (center) with Max and Ida at her seventy-fifth birthday
celebration

Stanley, circa 1991

Stanley and Victor
Mair (University of
Pennsylvania), 1992

Peter Fish, 1993

Stanley and Jane's house in Andes, New York, 1998

Stanley and Francis Cardinal George, archbishop of Chicago, 2003

Stanley and Henry Louis Gates, 2003

"Top of the World" Chicago condo, 2004

Stanley at Daemen College, 2014

Chapter 6

Top of the World:
The Windy City Years and Beyond

S tanley made his mind up for certain on July 1, 1998, while he was sitting in an airport lounge waiting to board a flight to Venice, where he was to visit an old friend and colleague, Jackson Cope. He had received the offer to come to the University of Illinois at Chicago (UIC) late in April and had been given until July 1—that very day—to decide. As usual, he had agonized over the decision: he knew he would enjoy the challenge, but he wasn't sure he wanted to move after all. And he was concerned that Jane would not be happy to leave Chapel Hill. A few minutes before he was to board the plane, he slipped his phone from his pocket, called Betsy Hoffman, and said, "Betsy, we've got a deal. Jane and I are coming to UIC." The provost was relieved and delighted. What a coup for her up-and-coming urban university. When Stanley returned from his week in Italy, he and Jane began the laborious process of planning their move to Chicago.

Over a period of four months, they searched for the perfect residence in Chicago, flying back and forth to the city to view properties. Finally, late in the process, they found it: a stylish condo in a twenty-one-story residential high-rise building less than a block from Lakeshore Drive and the magnificent Lake Michigan. Designed by Milton Schwartz and built in 1953, the building, 320 West Oakdale Avenue, was such an exemplar of the architectural style called "the International Style" that it was featured in several architectural and interior design books and magazines. The walls were ceiling-to-floor glass, and slabs of concrete on each floor projected far out beyond the glass walls, collectively appearing from street level and beyond like giant louvers. The interior was unique and especially elegant. The designer capitalized on the fact that there were no exterior walls, only glass, by constructing all of the rooms in an almost 360-degree circular core in the center of the apartment, leaving the spacious peripheral interiors as a kind of beautiful observation deck and living space overlooking the lake, Lincoln Park, and Chicago itself. The white walls and gleaming ash hardwood floors of the peripheral space lightened up the atmosphere considerably and provided the perfect venue for entertaining guests. Stanley would use this space to hold many formal receptions and fund-raising events. After attending a reception in the apartment, one scholar quipped, "Now I have experienced Michel Foucault's Panopticon: Stanley can observe all of Chicago without himself being seen." Stanley was on the top of the world.

He began his appointment as dean of the College of Liberal Arts and Sciences on January 1 and was also awarded joint appointments in the departments of English, political science, and criminal justice. The press made much of the fact that he had negotiated a salary of $230,000. While this salary may have seemed excessive to outsiders, it was not too out of line in 1999 for the chief executive officer of a large and complex college. What observers did not know, however, was that he had negotiated a deal like no other for a dean: he would not be required to work on evenings, weekends, and summers. This was unheard of in academic administration. Deans are expected to spend substantial time courting potential donors and entertaining past donors. Some appointment contracts specifically stipulate that the dean is expected to raise a certain amount of money in gifts per year or to have a certain number of contact hours each month with present and potential donors, and these efforts are typically transacted precisely during evenings, weekends, and summers. In addition, most deans are typically on call twenty-four hours a day because potential emergencies are always a possibility: a student commits suicide, a chemistry lab bursts into flames from a mishandled experiment, equipment is stolen from an office, a thorny personnel problem unexpectedly erupts and needs immediate attention. Stanley's arrangement was highly unusual, and perhaps even unprecedented.

UIC was a much different institution from the elite universities he had become accustomed to. As an urban, public university, a substantial portion of the student body was composed of students who were the first in their families to attend college. Many were first-generation

Americans from various ethnic backgrounds: Slavic, East Indian, Asian, Hispanic—a wide ethnic mix. Many lived in Chicago, held full-time jobs, and commuted to school. He found them to be hardworking and serious students who took education seriously. The undergraduates at Duke all looked to him as if nothing tragic had ever happened to them; the undergraduates at UIC all looked as if they had just seen something horrible in their neighborhoods the night before—and might well have. He found this difference in the student body to be a great attraction. UIC was an exciting institution to be a part of and to teach at, and he frequently spoke enthusiastically about the university, especially when recruiting new faculty.

He found the situation at UIC concerning academic reputation to be similar to what he had encountered at Duke—only more so. The Duke English department suffered from an inferiority complex, even though the institution had begun to think of itself as in the same league as the Southern Ivies like Emory and Vanderbilt. UIC had no pretension whatsoever to being elite in any way and suffered from its own inferiority complex. It existed in the shadow of (and in close proximity to) several prestigious universities, including Northwestern, DePaul, Loyola University Chicago, and the venerable University of Chicago—not to mention *the* University of Illinois in Urbana, the state's land grant university. He realized that the same prescription he used at Duke was called for: attract first-rate scholars in a number of disciplines that will put the institution on the map and generate substantial positive publicity and therefore excitement about the institution. His experience recruiting scholars at Duke had taught him an important lesson: if you are at an institution like UIC and wish to hire a real star in a discipline and have identified two people as being at the very top of that field—one with an appointment at Yale, the other with an appointment at, say, Michigan State—you have a substantially better chance of recruiting the faculty member from Yale. Why? Because if you've been at Yale or Harvard or Princeton, you have already made it to the big time. If you are at Michigan State, you are still on the upward ladder, and a position at UIC would seem to be a lateral move, if that. This insight paid off repeatedly for him. To the amazement of many, he successfully recruited the distinguished labor historian, Leon Fink, from the University of North Carolina, and both Gerald Graff and Sander Gilman from the University of Chicago.

In the first year and a half of his tenure as dean, he had hired thirty-eight new faculty members, including seven African American faculty. He even attempted unsuccessfully to attract his friend Houston Baker from Duke and Rita Dove, the Pulitzer Prize–winning poet, from the University of Virginia.

When Stanley heard that Rice University was courting his good friend and colleague from Johns Hopkins, Walter Benn Michaels, he immediately recognized an opportunity. Michaels's partner, Jennifer Ashton, taught American literature at Cornell, and the couple was finding the long-distance relationship to be onerous. Rice was able to interest them in positions and eventually made substantial offers to them. One evening, Stanley called Michaels. "Walter, is it true that you and Jennifer have received offers from Rice?" Michaels replied, "Yes, but I don't know if we will accept them or not. We're still considering the opportunity." After a short pause, Stanley said in a firm, measured voice, "Walter, it is acceptable, even admirable, to receive an offer from Rice, but it is completely unacceptable to *accept* that offer. *Many* of us have received offers from Rice, Walter, but none of us have *accepted* them. We would all be together if we had." Walter Benn Michaels was speechless. "I want you and Jennifer to come to UIC," Stanley continued. "I'll make it worth your while." From experience, Stanley knew that the key to closing this deal was to concentrate on recruiting Jennifer, so he pulled out all the stops and won them both over.

The rapid-fire hiring of these new faculty in a diversity of disciplines caused a great deal of positive press for UIC, both in the state and nationally. "Fish observers" smiled knowingly as they watched him duplicate his Duke hiring feats in the Windy City. In fact, one of his general goals—and the provost's for him, as well—was to dramatically raise the profile of the institution; he would certainly do that. His activities generated substantial publicity, especially for an institution that was routinely ignored by the local newspapers—the *Chicago Tribune* and the *Chicago Sun-Times*—both of which regularly paid close attention to the goings-on at the University of Illinois at Urbana. From 2001 to 2005 he served as a monthly columnist for the *Chronicle of Higher Education*, and many of his columns dealt with his life as a dean at UIC, so this too helped catapult the institution into the limelight. One prominent scholar at UIC pointed out that he would travel around the country giving papers, and colleagues at other institutions would say that they had no idea who their dean was but they sure knew who *his* dean was. While the *Sun-Times'* coverage seemed positive to Stanley and his initiatives from the beginning of his appointment, the *Tribune's* was at first quite critical, both in relation to his appointment and to his various initiatives, but the publication eventually warmed up—so much so that in 2003 it named him Chicagoan of the Year for Culture. In Stanley's mind, the hiring of celebrity academics and the generating of positive publicity were a means to an end: to lift the miasma of an inferiority complex, to help faculty collectively feel that they were part of an enterprise that was known and admired by others.

One of his first initiatives was to create a UIC faculty club. Elite universities often have faculty clubs, and at some institutions they can be quite swanky, featuring a full bar and high-quality dining in an upscale atmosphere. Stanley had loved the old faculty club known as the John Hopkins Club and felt that such gathering places did much to promote an atmosphere of community and collegiality. He made his case and eventually convinced central administration to convert a rudimentary lounge in the Behavioral Sciences Building into a modest but attractive faculty club, complete with a lounge with a bar and a small fireplace, a casual dining area, and a formal dining area with white linen tablecloths and windows on two sides. It was a warm and pleasant setting to meet friends and colleagues. On the day the club opened, Stanley walked over to inspect it. A small crowd had already gathered, and as he strode into the room, the crowd burst into applause. The club would do much to improve morale over the years.

Another of Stanley's initiatives was to create a regular, informal meeting of the deans. Every two weeks the Council of Deans met formally in the chancellor and provost's conference room with an agenda set by the provost, but Stanley felt that a separate meeting was called for where the deans could meet in private to air their concerns and strategize. He was quickly emerging as a leader among the deans, but he understood that he was not the only leader; he shared that distinction with the powerful dean of medicine, Gerald Moss (who had served as the chair of the search committee that had brought Stanley to UIC). So Stanley cultivated his relationship with Moss, and together the two deans convened all the other deans in their own private meetings where they would prepare issues to bring to the attention of the provost. This strategy enabled the deans to talk with one voice on key issues that were to be presented to the provost and chancellor.

As part of her arrangement to come to UIC, Jane chose to be appointed to the College of Education rather than to the English department, which was part of the College of Liberal Arts and Sciences—Stanley's college. She reasoned that she had become more of an "education type" over the last few years and had radically changed her views of the academy. Her professional ambitions had finally been satisfied while at Duke: she was a full professor, her books *Sensational Designs* and *West of Everything* were well received, she was frequently invited to give talks and presentations across the nation, she was part of the power couple that everyone talked about. She had arrived. But living in the fast lane had exacted a heavy price. She increasingly became disillusioned with the agonistic—even cutthroat—atmosphere of the academy, where it seemed mandatory to attack colleagues' work at conferences and in articles. One semester while still at Duke she found herself scheduled to give lectures on different subjects in five universities while also teaching two reading-intensive graduate courses. The stress was overwhelming. She began to experience migraine headaches. To combat them she tried massage therapy and long walks in the woods. She was very unhappy. Perhaps the fast lane is not for everyone. She changed her appointment to half time, and for a few years she even considered leaving the academy altogether. Nothing seemed to work. Then she began to pay less attention to scholarly work and threw herself into her teaching, where she discovered an intense joy in a kind of experimental teaching that was more collaborative than traditional lectures. The students came alive, and so did she. This had been a major life transformation for her, so she believed she would be happy with an appointment in the College of Education.

Before arriving in Chicago, she developed a serious case of chronic fatigue syndrome, which caused her to sit out the first year. When she finally felt well enough to begin work, she was assigned an office next to the office of Bill Ayers, who in the 1960s had cofounded the Weather Underground, a leftist group that bombed public buildings in protest of the Vietnam War, and who became the focus of controversy during the 2008 presidential campaign when the Republicans attempted to associate him with Barack Obama in order to paint Obama as a countercultural radical. Despite colleagues like Ayers, she soon discovered that the College of Education was not a good fit after all. She found it hard to make friendships with her new colleagues, and she continued to suffer from her illness. As her second year was drawing to a close, she realized that a radical change was called for. She decided that she would try to convince central administration to give her a job renovating the physical spaces on campus to make them more livable for students. The campus had been designed by the great urban architect Walter Netsch, who had won awards for the UIC design, and most of the campus had been built in the 1960s and early 1970s. Jane felt that while the campus did have an industrial aesthetic and as such had aesthetic integrity (as opposed to the many college campuses that are a hodgepodge of many often conflicting architectural types), functionally the design was lacking. There were few places for students to sit down or lounge, which is particularly important for a university with a large number of commuter students. She felt that the physical atmosphere on the campus was so oppressive that it drained people's energy and morale.

She arranged to have lunch with Charlotte "Toby" Tate, who was serving as interim provost while the university conducted a national search that would culminate in hiring a replacement for Betsy Hoffman, who had taken a position at another university. Jane enthusiastically described her vision of how the campus could be transformed little by little. The administration decided to give her a chance, and the provost allocated $100,000 toward the project. Jane plunged into the project. Her first project would be the creation of a student lounge in the imposing Behavioral Sciences Building—the very building where Stanley had created his faculty club. She held focus groups with students and others and involved classes in the planning. Construction companies and retailers gave her special discounts, and before long she had created a beautiful and functional student lounge. She took an open, unused space and installed a square of lighting, carpeting, a comfortable sofa and chairs, and some potted plants, but the touch that made it special was the original artwork on the walls. "Nothing changes a space faster than original art," she said proudly to Stanley one evening. She had convinced two professors of advanced painting in the School of Art and Design to enlist their best graduate student painters to contribute works for an art exhibit.

Then Jane assembled a committee of judges to select five paintings that she bought for permanent display. She had transformed a dark, gloomy void into a warm, welcoming space. Jane organized a grand opening reception, complete with flowers, balloons, refreshments, and a music trio. The chancellor and other dignitaries attended.

When the chancellor discovered to her amazement that Jane was able to accomplish this feat for a mere $5,000, she was sold. Jane was appointed with the title of Assistant to the Provost for Campus Environment and would go on to create seventeen student lounges and a large project: a glassed-in faculty/student lounge and café spanning the first and second floors of the administration building and financed in part by a million dollar grant from a donor. Then she was assigned to renovate classrooms. She enlisted the help of a class of architecture and industrial arts students to come up with designs and a class in graphic arts that designed banners for the entire campus.

Jane may well have gotten disillusioned with scholarly work, but Stanley managed to continue his scholarship unabated throughout his tenure as dean. In 1999 Harvard University Press published *The Trouble with Principle*, a collection of sixteen essays along with a prologue and epilogue; five of the essays had not been previously published. While the chapters address a range of subjects, they are connected by a controlling thesis: Fundamental to liberal political philosophy is the belief that a just society is founded on such principles as "fairness" and "freedom," principles that supposedly exist independent of any specific context. Such abstract principles are thought to be capable of being defined in ways that enable them to remain free from partisan agendas and, consequently, are thought to be capable of serving as the foundation of legal decisions and political policies that favor no particular person or group but that respect all people and groups generally. Such efforts may be well intentioned, but in Stanley's view they are doomed to fail because whoever at the moment happens to be defining "fairness" or "mutual respect" or any other such principle will necessarily be doing so from a specific context, which includes that person's personal system of belief and values. It is impossible to rise above your context in order to fill in the content of so-called neutral principles. A general principle such as fairness, then, can be (and often is) deployed as a weapon in political and legal struggles because it conceals the interestedness of those appealing to it and obscures the fact that the actual policy, law, or proposal being advanced in the name of the principle is embedded in specific historical circumstances and furthers the objectives and interests of one set of individuals over and against those of others. The fact that general principles in effect do not exist but nonetheless can be deployed to effect harm may seem to be a contradiction, but Stanley argues that there is no contradiction in asserting that, on the one hand, general principles do not exist (that they have no substance except when they are invoked and thus invested with a specific substance that promotes a specific agenda) and that, on the other hand, they can be used to further odious agendas (that is, agendas that you yourself find to be odious). It is exactly the emptiness of principles (the fact that they can mean anything and thus nothing and therefore do not exist in any meaningful way *as neutral principles*) that makes them available to be used to do destructive (or productive) work in the world. Stanley dedicated his book to his close friend and Duke colleague Barbara Herrnstein Smith.

That same year, Blackwell published *The Stanley Fish Reader*, edited by H. Aram Veeser, a collection of eleven of Stanley's representative works, each headed by a short introduction written by a prominent scholar, including Judith Butler, Gerald Graff, Geoffrey Galt Harpham, and Steven Mailloux. Two years later, in 2001, Harvard University Press published *How Milton Works*, a collection of ten previously published works on Milton's poetry and prose, plus five new chapters, an introductory essay, and an epilogue.

While Stanley's tenure as dean was highly successful in the beginning, a series of events eventually soured the experience. Early in Stanley's tenure, the UIC chancellor, David C. Broski, left to become president of Bradley University. Then Stanley's boss and biggest supporter, Betsy Hoffman, left the institution to become the president of the University of Colorado system. The new chancellor, Sylvia Manning, appointed Robert Michael Tanner as the new provost, who would begin his appointment on July 1, 2002. He was an electrical and computer engineering specialist who prided himself on his love and knowledge of the arts and humanities: he knew Spanish and was fluent in French; he played the piano and classical guitar; and he was an aficionado of art, theater, and opera. When Stanley went to meet the new provost in his official capacity, they greeted one another before sitting down, and, in an attempt

141

to demonstrate his support of the humanities—and thus Stanley—he began to say something about Jacques Derrida, the father of deconstruction. Stanley cut him off and said, "Let's not go in that direction." The provost was immediately offended. Stanley was attempting to avert an intellectual argument with his new boss but had made a monumental blunder: he should have simply let the provost demonstrate his interest in the subject and then politely moved on to more official business. The damage was done: they had clashed immediately and would continue to have a rocky relationship. While there is no evidence that Tanner held the original incident against his dean, he had offered Stanley the opportunity to establish a constructive relationship and Stanley had in effect declined. Stanley never forgave himself for his faux pas.

Compounding the unease between the two was the fact that the provost soon discovered that Stanley was not working within his budget and in fact had racked up a huge deficit—a dean's greatest mortal sin. These were very difficult years for public universities across the nation, and many institutions faced stiff budget cuts. Once during a meeting of the deans of arts and sciences who were members of the Committee on Institutional Cooperation—an organization of the presidents, provosts, and deans of the Big Ten Universities plus the University of Chicago established to share ideas and resources for their mutual benefit—Stanley announced to colleague deans that he was on the outs with his provost because he had amassed a deficit of six million dollars. The actual debt was closer to double that amount. Tanner gave Stanley a piece of his mind about the college's finances and negotiated an arrangement with the college whereby he would relieve a certain portion of the debt and in return the college would follow a very specific five-year plan to pay off the remaining debt. The previous administration had given Stanley free rein; now it was time to pay the bill.

The last three years of his tenure as dean were nothing like the first two. Once Betsy Hoffman and Chancellor Broski had left, he no longer had the kind of support system that he originally enjoyed. They had given him relative free rein over the college, and the institution had sufficient resources to allow him to begin to build the college's reputation. This would not last. Public universities across the nation had already begun to experience fiscal crises when the September 11, 2001, terrorist attacks on the Pentagon and the World Trade Center occurred, killing nearly three thousand people and plunging the nation into a prolonged crisis and a major economic downturn. Suddenly, as a state and federal priority, higher education took a back seat to other more pressing concerns. State funding for universities began to plummet, and public institutions began to tighten their budgetary belts. Stanley would not be afforded the opportunity to take advantage of the momentum that he had generated in the college, and the rest of his tenure would be a series of frustrations.

Never a stranger to controversy, he became embroiled in a well-publicized feud with members of the state legislature—usually a serious misstep for any college administrator, even a university president. In fact, some university presidents forbid deans and vice presidents from interacting with legislators without prior approval; angering the wrong legislator can potentially have serious consequences, since legislators typically have the final say on the level of funding that the institution will receive. Immediately following the 9/11 attacks, in November of 2001, the state of Illinois, suffering economically, ordered all public agencies to return 1 percent of their budgets—a huge blow to UIC. And then, in 2002, the state faced a severe budget shortfall, which, among other things, led to the first cuts to university budgets in a decade. State support for UIC during 2002 and 2003 was cut by $54 million on top of many millions in midyear "give backs" of already allocated funds. A Republican state legislator, Steve Rauschenberger, who had long been a critic of higher education in the state, took aim at UIC, and specifically at Stanley's efforts to recruit what the legislator termed "rock star academics" at the expense of undergraduate education. Chair of the powerful Senate Appropriations Committee, Rauschenberger was especially upset by reports in the local press that Stanley was not only hiring some professors at six-figure salaries but was often sweetening the deal with lucrative signing bonuses and summer stipends. It was revealed that Walter Benn Michaels not only negotiated a salary of $175,000 but also a $58,000 summer stipend. The deal also included a salary and stipend for his partner. The legislator believed that such seemingly profligate spending was unseemly given the state's fiscal crisis and that UIC should abandon its goal to become one of the best urban research universities in the nation and concentrate instead on educating undergraduates for the workforce.

In response, Stanley took aim in his *Chronicle of Higher Education* column, in an essay titled "The End of Innocence," first at the *Chicago Tribune* (for muckraking) and then at politicians for attempting to force fiscal restraint on universities without first obtaining the facts about how universities work in the first place. He even mentioned Illinois State Governor Rod Blagojevich (though not by name), who during his gubernatorial campaign had repeatedly promised that as governor he would end the fiscal extravagance of the state's universities. The *Tribune*'s new higher education reporter had made a massive public records request of UIC officials, a fishing expedition that resulted in an article questioning whether UIC was being a good steward of public funds. It cited several expensive trips taken by university trustees and a number of restaurant reimbursements for faculty and administrators, highlighting one meal in particular: a dinner costing $419 at an exclusive Chicago restaurant, Spiaggia, that Stanley had with Jane and three visiting professors.

Senator Rauschenberger continued his campaign, saying that he was going to look into the signing bonuses and other deal sweeteners that Stanley was using to recruit faculty. The legislator was quoted as saying, "Let them teach at Stanford," meaning that faculty who demanded exorbitant salaries need not come to UIC. In response, Stanley telephoned the lawmaker and asked if he had been quoted correctly. "Do you really *not* want UIC to recruit the best and brightest professors?" he asked the legislator. The two then engaged in what turned out to be a productive discussion about institutional priorities and reputations. Rauschenberger later commented to the press that while he did not believe he and Stanley had arrived at a meeting of the minds, at least the dean was interested in his perspective.

Then, in December of 2003, the Illinois Board of Higher Education, perhaps in an attempt to mollify legislators, announced that it would commission a major study of faculty productivity in the state's universities. The board would empanel a committee to study all facets of faculty productivity, including course loads and research levels in each university. This announcement angered faculty throughout the state, who saw the initiative as improper interference in the affairs of faculty and as a thinly veiled effort to force them to teach more. This was the last straw for Stanley. He had just announced the week before that he would step down from his position as dean once his term had ended at the end of June 2004. He had become exceedingly frustrated by the ongoing financial crisis and the legislature's inability or unwillingness to fund the state's universities at a level he deemed appropriate. He was also not certain that the provost would choose to renew his appointment for another term, and he certainly did not want to find out. He had been a terrible pain to the provost, so much so that had their positions been reversed, he might very well have removed himself from office. Now that his resignation was widely publicized, he took it upon himself to condemn the state board. He told a *Tribune* reporter, "Either they don't have the slightest idea how higher education works on the research level—or they do know what it takes, and they have set out to destroy it." This statement was republished in news reports throughout the state. Had he not already announced his resignation, he may well have faced removal from office for such brazen criticism of the very board that oversees the state universities. Many deans have been fired for saying far less.

When Stanley let it be known that he was stepping down as dean, Jerry Graff and a few other scholars quietly met with the provost and attempted to convince him to find a way to keep Stanley on as dean, but they were not successful. The newspapers covered his decision extensively. While he did not publicly link his decision to the diminishing state funding of universities, his frustration with the state was by then well known. He did say to reporters at the time that further reductions in state support would completely erase the gains UIC had made over the previous four years, which included being listed for the first time by the National Science Foundation as one of the top fifty U.S. universities in federal funding. As a tribute, the university named him Distinguished Professor, the college conferred the title of Dean Emeritus on him as a gesture of appreciation for all that he had done for the college, and the Institute for Humanities named a biennial lecture series in his honor. The first lecturer was Fredric Jameson, followed by Stephen Greenblatt, Judith Butler, and Slavoj Žižek. A wealthy donor funded the series, and Stanley and Jane are invited as distinguished guests to the biennial event and to have dinner with the lecturer.

For three years while he was dean, he had given talks and seminars at Northwestern University's law school. David E. Van Zandt, the law school dean, repeatedly called him during that time and attempted to lure him to take a permanent position there. Stanley had always declined.

After he decided to resign his deanship, he called Van Zandt one day and said, "David, I'd like to come to Northwestern Law School after all." As luck would have it, the dean had already used the funds to make another appointment. It was too late for Stanley. Had he been able to secure that position, he would have been quite satisfied to stay in Chicago in his top-of-the-world condo. And he already had many friends at the law school, but it was not to be.

He would join the English department for one year after his deanship, in part to give Jane one more year to complete her renovation projects. When he first arrived at UIC, his administrative assistant had arranged for Stanley to have a second office on the same floor as the English department. She was a very powerful personality, one of those staff assistants in the university who had been at the institution seemingly forever and had more influence than anybody would ever guess. It was a huge corner office on the nineteenth floor and was decorated quite nicely. He rarely used it as dean, but it was a welcome perk when he left the dean's office and returned to the faculty. He did not mind teaching his classes that year as a faculty member, but it just didn't feel right to him. His office door was always open, but colleagues rarely stopped by to talk, and he began to think that he just did not want to hang around the university any longer as a faculty member. He was bored yet again.

With the Northwestern position off the table and the faculty position in the English department not a good fit, he decided to find a position in Florida. In 1997 Jane and he had bought a lovely house in Delray Beach. They had got it at a good price and had rented it out over the intervening years. In the middle of his year on the UIC faculty in 2005, he turned to Jane and said, "We've got our wonderful house in Delray. Let's move to Florida, fix the house up, and I'll try to find some position there." Jane agreed. They still had their beautiful home in the Catskills, and in 2009 they would also purchase a smart apartment in New York City on Ninth Street below Fifth Avenue near Washington Square.

The two most likely Florida institutions to offer him an appointment were Florida Atlantic University and Florida International University. He already had a relationship with Florida Atlantic University (FAU). Over the years he had given several talks there, and in the late 1990s had been offered a chaired university professorship called the Schmidt Scholar. He had turned it down. Then in 2003 he had been a finalist for president of the university. He had been nominated for the presidency in the early fall of 2002 and had agreed to be considered, promptly sending in his application materials. He heard nothing from the search committee for several months, so he assumed that the committee was not interested in his candidacy. Then, during the last week of January he received a call from a reporter with the *Palm Beach Post* asking for his reaction to being named one of the five finalists for the presidency. He had no idea that he was still a viable candidate, much less a semifinalist. "My reaction?" he barked at the reporter, "This is news to me!" The reporter revealed the names of the five candidates to Stanley. One was the recently reelected lieutenant governor of the state, Frank Brogan. Word had it that the Republican elite had informed Brogan that he was not going to be the next governor of the state, even though he was lieutenant governor, but they had found a respectable spot for him as president of FAU. Brogan, then forty-nine years old, had no doctorate, only a master's degree in education, nor had he any experience as a college teacher or administrator. Something was not right, Stanley thought to himself. He needed some inside information, some advice.

He had known the then-president of Florida International University, Modesto "Mitch" Maidique, for some years, so he dialed his private cell phone. Maidique, who was traveling abroad at the time, took the call. "Mitch, Stanley. I've got to tell you about this situation." He repeated what the reporter had told him. The president knew the candidates and claimed to know what was going to happen. He predicted that in the end it would come down to Stanley and the lieutenant governor and that Stanley only had a 5 percent chance of being appointed president.

Never one to give up easily, he decided to go through with the process despite what appeared to be a predetermined outcome. He went through the formal interviews, and he loved the experience. He enjoyed the meetings, appreciated the many faculty and staff he met with, and came to develop a very positive feeling for the institution. By the time he returned to Chicago from the days of interviews, he knew that he had wowed everyone and that he would be one of the three finalists. He was right. The committee announced the three candidates on January 24: Brogan, Stanley, and Thomas Hanley, the dean of engineering at the University of Louisville.

Stanley was glad to have been named a finalist, but he was becoming increasingly skeptical. The chair of the search committee contacted him to describe the process going forward. He would be expected to spend nearly an entire week in Florida. Monday through Thursday would be devoted to visiting the institution's many branch campuses and talking with constituents; the search committee would meet on that Friday to make a final decision, and then on Friday night there would be a banquet announcing the final choice. Something was very wrong. "Well, how can there be a banquet announcing your choice on that very same day?" he asked the committee chair. "Doesn't the job have to be offered, and then the person who is offered the job would have a certain amount of time to consider it, and then enter into negotiations and arrive at an acceptable agreement before an announcement is made?" Without skipping a beat, the chair replied, "Oh, we always assume that the person who is offered a desirable position like this will take the job." At that moment, Stanley knew that his friend Mitch was right: the fix had always been in. Complicating matters was the fact that the week when he would be expected to be in Florida coincided with one of the most important times in every dean's annual schedule: the annual budget planning meetings where the dean makes the case for the level of funding that the college would receive over the next year. Well, he thought to himself, if this FAU candidacy is a sham, not real, my college's budget presentations to the provost and his people are very real. I refuse to waste my time. After thinking about his prospects for three days, he grabbed the phone, dialed the committee chair, and officially withdrew his candidacy.

At least I gave them something to reflect on, he thought to himself. He had explained in depth to the search committee the difference between a university that is simply doing the job and one that is on the move to another level. "It's very simple," he explained. "In the first, the job is being done, instruction is serious and competent and well informed, the students are being educated. In the second, these same things are occurring, but the faculty is itself producing the texts that are being studied at other universities. That's the difference. You've got a faculty, in whatever departments there are, where at other universities their research or their interpretations are the ones that other professors have to take into consideration." He had told the search committee that this would be his priority were he to be appointed.

So, years after he had withdrawn as a finalist for president, FAU remained one possibility for a post-deanship appointment, but so was Florida International University (FIU). He had given a well-received commencement address there some years earlier, and, of course, he was on good terms with the president and others on campus. After discussions with officials on both campuses, Stanley received similar offers from both. As usual, he agonized over the decision and then finally accepted the position at Florida Atlantic. He had reasoned that FAU was only about a fifteen-minute drive from his house, while Florida International was a nearly two-hour grueling drive into traffic-congested Miami, but now that he had made the decision, he felt quite uneasy about what he had done. He mentioned his unease to one of his associate deans, who said, "Look, Stan, you don't want to make your decision about employment on the basis of which campus is closer to your house. That just doesn't make sense." Stanley instantly realized that his advisor was right. This was advice he himself would have given anybody else, but, of course, it is sometimes much easier to give advice to others than to see how that same advice applies to your own life circumstances. He picked up the phone and called the FIU provost and asked, "Is it too late to change my mind." To Stanley's amazement, the provost replied, "No, and I'll raise your salary from $50,000 to $80,000." Stanley had ended up with the perfect situation: a chaired position—he would be the Davidson-Kahn Distinguished University Professor of Humanities and Law—at a respectable salary, with few duties, teaching only one course a year.

Jane and Stanley had discovered Delray Beach during one of their many trips to visit Max and Ida in Pompano Beach, where the retirees owned a condo. The resort town of then about sixty thousand residents is located on the Atlantic Ocean in Palm Beach County and is a bustling seaside village of upscale bistros and shops. Flowing banners on streetlight poles proudly announce the town's slogan: "Florida's Village by the Sea." Throughout the year tourists flock to the village to visit its stunningly beautiful beaches, shop in the trendy boutiques, and take in games at the Delray Beach International Tennis Championships. Delray is decidedly not a typical "beach bum" community. Sipping a cocktail in one of the many outdoor cafes, you would likely see at least one of every luxury car made: BMW sedans, Mercedes convertibles, Bentleys, a Rolls Royce or two. Cadillacs seem positively low class in Delray Beach.

The "beautiful people," all half naked except for designer beachwear and sporting $1,000 designer sunglasses and diamond-encrusted Rolex watches, hardly seem to notice the oppressive heat and thick humidity during their leisurely strolls along Atlantic Avenue, the town's main street, which dead-ends at the seashore. Exclusive condos and posh gated communities of homes painted in bright pastels are nestled among swaying palms and lush tropical vegetation. In 2012 Rand McNally named Delray "the most fun small town in America."

Jane and Stanley's home is a typical one-story "Florida house" less than a city block from the shore. One of only four homes on a tiny cul-de-sac named Sandpiper Lane, the yellow stucco home with white trim features multipaned windows lining several of the rooms. It is a comfortable home with hardwood floors and bright, spacious rooms. Jane's grand piano dominates the living room, and beautiful French doors open onto Stanley's office. The landscaping is magnificent. Jane had taken a bare yard and created a private Garden of Eden, thick with flowers, tropical plants, and stately palms—complete with a lily pond and waterfall fountain. The lush landscaping has the effect of walling in the property, creating a serenely private sanctuary. Jane and Stanley had created a tropical Shangri-la. They would spend the winters in Florida and the summers in the Catskills, occasionally visiting their apartment in Manhattan.

They moved into their Delray home in 2005. Jane had officially retired that year. She was 65 years old and was still plagued by illness, and she later survived a horrific automobile accident. During the next decade Stanley was quite productive. In 2006 he began to pen a regular column for the *New York Times*, and he continued to give many public lectures. He also published several important books. Oxford University Press published his controversial *Save the World on Your Own Time* in 2008. In it, he continues and extends his thesis from 1995's *Professional Correctness*, attacking the increasingly more widespread practice of professors' fashioning their curricula in such a way as to advance their own political agendas. Progressive professors nationwide construed this book as a declaration of war on their entire professional raison d'*être*.

The University of Pennsylvania Press published his first work of cultural criticism in 2011: *The Fugitive in Flight: Faith, Liberalism, and Law in a Classic TV Show*. A labor of love, this is a penetrating examination of the popular television drama *The Fugitive* that aired from 1963 to 1967. Stanley had always been fascinated with the series. Since early in his career he had a habit of having the television on when he wrote his scholarly works—another habit that scandalized many other academicians. Often a baseball game would drone on in the background, and he would keep an eye on the television set as he wrote, but once an episode of *The Fugitive* came on (reruns continued to air for decades), all other activity stopped. Jane would saunter into the room to ask him to do something for her; discover that *The Fugitive* was on the television; linger for a while, attracted by the film noir dialogue and cinematography; and then turn on her heels and walk out. She knew better than to disturb him when this one series was on. He was transfixed. On a whim, he began to take notes on five-by-eight cards as he studied each episode. He eventually accumulated thousands of note cards. Then he began to construct theses about what was going on in the plot. He was hooked. The book that resulted from this analysis was well received.

That same year, 2011, HarperCollins published a book that would become a best seller and was perhaps the only noncontroversial book the enfant terrible ever wrote: *How to Write a Sentence: And How to Read One*. Not a manual, not a handbook, not a textbook, this slim volume is a "meditation"—a careful and thoughtful reflection on prose style. He approaches his subject as a self-confessed connoisseur: "Some appreciate fine art; others appreciate fine wines. I appreciate fine sentences." Rather than disseminating "how to" knowledge, he exposes readers to a sensibility—a consciousness of and sensitivity to style. He focuses on sentences—rather than, say, words or paragraphs or essays—because the sentence is the basic building block of all discourse, the basic unit by which we make a statement about the world. Words by themselves contain the *potential* to represent thought in the form of discourse, but independent of their arrangement in a coherent sentence, they are only that—potential elements of discourse. Syntax—the meaningful relationship of words to one another—is what confers on those words the ability to convey meaning. This book was so successful that the publisher immediately offered him a lucrative contract for a book on how to construct arguments.

In the following year, 2012, Cambridge University Press published *Versions of Antihumanism: Milton and Others*. This book is a collection of essays, some previously published, about the works of Milton (primar-ily), as well as Herbert, Jonson, Marvell, Donne, and Hobbes. These are typical Stanley Fish tour de force close readings of some of these authors' works. Two years later the University of Chicago Press published his *Versions of Academic Freedom: From Professionalism to Revolution*. This book explores the way people talk about a key concept in the academic world: academic freedom. He is especially interested in the assumptions that people make when they discuss this subject—assumptions about the nature of truth, the purpose of education, and the social and political functions of the academy. In the book, he categorizes ways of conceiv-ing of academic freedom into a taxonomy of five schools, and then he illustrates how all but one school is lacking: the school that understands academic freedom, not as an overarching freedom that protects any and every instance of speech of someone who just happens to be a professor, but as a freedom of narrow constraint on speech pertaining to the specific kinds of scholarly work that academics do—a freedom of professional inquiry within the limited bounds of a professional discipline.

One day early in 2015 Stanley was working on his next book, a col-lection of his *New York Times* columns that Princeton University Press was planning to publish later that year. He sat back in his chair and watched his cat play with a catnip toy on the hardwood floor. The Florida winds had kicked up, and the palms and other vegetation in the courtyard outside the French doors began to sway furiously. A storm was moving through. He began to think of that day in 1977 when he and Jane, in a desperate attempt to escape their pain after leaving their spouses, had jumped into his Mercedes and headed toward Florida—a land where they could forget their troubles, at least for a short while. He reflected on his life for a brief moment. He knew all too well that, had he not found his way into college, he would have gotten stuck for life in some job in Providence, most likely running Max's business. He realized how fortunate he had been. He had attended one of the finest high schools in the nation and had prepared himself well for college—almost in spite of himself. Except for that rocky first year in graduate school, he had sailed through college and graduate school. He had begun his career at Berkeley, a respectable—if, at that time, up and coming—English department. He had revolutionized thinking not only in Milton scholarship but in a much larger arena. And he had gone on to have a storied career. He wondered briefly if Max would have approved. Then he thought of Adrienne. He genuinely cared for her, but his life with her had become untenable. He had found in Jane a soul mate. A real intellectual.

He recalled the trip Jane and he had taken that fateful day when they had, figuratively, eloped to Florida, and he remembered the sunglasses he had lost on the side of the highway outside of Savannah. He remembered finding the crushed glasses on his return trip to Baltimore and his attempt to interpret meaning from the shattered glass.

The wind suddenly died down, and Jane came into the room with a cup of steaming tea. He had made the right decision.

Chapter 7

Stan the Man:
Terrible, or Not *Terrible*

Observers have always found Stanley difficult to characterize. His reputation as an enfant terrible might be warranted in part, but perhaps not fully. Those who despise him perceive him to be a combatant preoccupied with winning every argument at any cost; a sophist who will argue a position to win, even if he does not believe what he is arguing; a contrarian who revels in verbal combat simply for its own sake; a loud, cigar-smoking bully; a smug, arrogant narcissist; an unrepentant publicity hound. David Lodge's fictional character Morris Zapp, loosely fashioned after Stanley, did much to reinforce and popularize this image. A cynical operator devoid of intellectual and moral principles, Zapp craves power and desires to dominate people. He is a jet-setting academic superstar who drives expensive sports cars and lusts after money—and colleagues' wives.

Even Stanley's supporters can find him infuriating at times. Sometimes he can tune colleagues out. He will be socializing with friends and a colleague will want to discuss his own recent scholarship, and Stanley will interrupt and announce that he doesn't like to talk shop. At dinner with colleagues he would rather talk about cars, basketball, or real estate prices than intellectual issues. But as with the David Lodge character, these descriptions, while they do contain some elements of truth, are a caricature of a much more complex person. Those who know him well tell a different tale.

Repeatedly, supporters will praise his intellectual integrity and his fearlessness. What seems to some to be senseless combativeness in reality is a compulsion to set things straight about an issue. When he senses a flaw in someone's reasoning, he is eager—or compelled—to engage that person and to point out how he believes the issue should be understood. He argues hard and refuses to tolerate shabby thinking; he has a nose for it. He carefully watches someone he is arguing with to detect weak arguments and is skilled at perceiving those weaknesses. If you want to argue with Stanley, you had better know what you are going to say and be prepared to support it with facts and solid reasoning. He demands a persuasive argument, one that is coherent, internally consistent, and that has a conceptual frame in which evidence leads to a logical conclusion, not just an airy theory or an unsupported assertion. If you make an assertion of fact, he expects you to support it with ample evidence. When he points out the flaws in an interlocutor's reasoning, some interpret this as rude and disrespectful, whereas he understands himself to be setting the record straight. For him, intellectual disputes are a serious business and demand meticulousness and intellectual integrity and should never be confused with being polite to people. In this way, he is a true intellectual; he has an uncompromising attitude toward how arguments are made, claims asserted, and evidence marshaled.

An oft-repeated story illustrates this point. In the early 1980s he attended a conference on law and literature held at the University of Minnesota. The conference was focused on legal interpretation and the tensions between objectivity and political bias, and many of the attendees were philosophers. Stanley sat in the audience intently taking in presentation after presentation. Finally, he had had enough. He had been listening to a panel of philosophers discuss interpretation. As soon as the question-and-answer session began, he took the floor and informed the panelists that they had no idea what they were talking about. They were simply repeating clichés and fallacies that everyone was familiar with. This was a devastating comment from the floor issued in a confrontational way. The philosophers were stunned and had no idea who he was. He had blindsided them. He went on to inform them that not only could he explain why they were wrong, he could make a better case for their own argument than they had. In the exchange that followed, the panelists would make assertions that Stanley would then demolish with a barrage of cogent arguments bolstered by specific references to the work of other scholars. One commentator likened the session to a series of sucker punches. After the session, a colleague asked him, "Stanley do you feel bad about what just happened?" Stanley looked puzzled, replying, "Are you kidding? Why would I feel bad? They had it all wrong. *Someone* needed to point that out."

His need to set the record straight is a manifestation of his larger need to impose order on his world. Some would say that he has a touch of obsessive-compulsive disorder. He always keeps his desk and workspace neat and orderly; he does not like to leave the house for a trip if it is not in apple-pie order; and he hates to see a picture hook hammered into the wall because he cringes at the drywall being punctured, so he arranges to be out of the house when pictures are hung. He finds great pleasure in maintaining things around the house. One reason that Jane and he could comfortably maintain three residences is that he is always on top of things at all three homes. He might be in Delray but he would be telephoning their handyman in the Catskills to have him paint the porch furniture, and then he would be calling the air conditioning contractors in New York City to have them replace the air conditioning unit in their apartment. Ten minutes later he would be calling a service in Delray to have them reupholster the arms on a chair in their sunroom. He's always thinking about organizing the maintenance at all three homes. Those who know him well smile with amusement that he loves to vacuum. Jane and he have no fewer than three vacuum cleaners in each of their residences. Once when he and Jane were living in Baltimore and were preparing to leave for a cross-country trip, Stanley began to vacuum the carpets when the vacuum cleaner stopped working properly. Despite the fact that they were leaving for the airport on a tight schedule, Stanley insisted on taking the vacuum cleaner to the repair shop first, thereby potentially jeopardizing their effort to make their plane on time. And, of course, he meticulously maintains his cars, regularly taking them in to the mechanic to make sure that everything is shipshape.

Some close to him speculate that his obsessive attention to order and cleanliness is psychologically a reaction against the turmoil of the Fish family home, where his mother would scream and rant and he and his siblings would shout back in response. His was a childhood of chaos, cacophony, discord, and messiness. He seems to have an internal need for order, neatness, and a sense of control over his surroundings, as if he is perpetually battling the chaos of his youth.

Much of his psychology derives from his chaotic relationship with his mother, Ida. In many ways, they were very much alike: headstrong, combative, indomitable, unyielding, supremely self-confident, unwilling to suffer fools. He even resembles his mother, just as his brother Ron resembles Max, his father. But Ida and Stanley were like two firecrackers that would set one another off. There was just too much fire in each of them to expect them to coexist harmoniously. Their contentiousness is what drove him as a young man to leave home as soon as he could. As he left for Penn, he took his brother Ron aside and advised him to leave home as soon as he was able; years later, the two brothers would give the same advice to their younger brother Peter. Their sister, Rita, probably had it the toughest of anyone. She had to live among three testosterone-filled boys, an emotionally absent father, and a mother whom everyone termed a terror. Even late in life, when Max had passed away and Ida lived in Florida, Jane and Stanley would visit, and Ida would bicker with her son unrelentingly. His explosive family home life and his on-going combat with his mother molded Stanley in substantial ways. He would end up marrying someone equally strong willed, difficult, and opinionated as his mother, prolonging his own suffering for two decades before finally extracting himself from his first marriage. All his life he preferred to dine out rather than eat at home. When Jane started living with Stanley, she at first took his reluctance to eat at home personally, as if it were a statement about her cooking prowess. More likely, it is something much deeper: a negative association of eating at home with sitting around the family dining-room table as a child and launching into yet another chaotic fight with his mother. Dining in the Fish family home was always tumultuous.

So, his compulsion to set the record straight and to do so with a clean, orderly argument that sweeps away the messy thinking of his op-ponents and his need to maintain a neat, tidy environment and to avoid familial chaos are quite likely an attempt to escape the pandemonium that was Ida's world.

This compulsion to set the record straight is often combined with a kind of intellectual fearlessness. He is happy to attend a conference of adherents to one way of seeing the world and gleefully stand up and explain to them how they have got it all wrong. His stance in *Professional Correctness* and *Save the World on Your Own Time* in which he excoriates those in English studies who attempt to make their work effect change in the world was guaranteed from the start to alienate the vast majority of professors in English studies, since a whole generation or two had dedicated themselves to doing just that. Although he was arguing from a theoretically principled position and making a coherent argument about the disciplinary integrity of English studies, many in the field understood his position to be a right-wing attack on progressive intellectual work, which was especially ironic since it was Stanley himself who, while at Duke, was at the forefront of the progressive movement that squared off against the National Association of Scholars to combat the conservative attack on progressive trends in intellectual work being embraced in the universities.

Those who served under him in administrative capacities report an identical kind of fearlessness. He would think nothing of giving a piece of his mind to any of his superiors, be they his provost, the university president, or even state legislators. To him, the point at hand was always more important than any negative consequence that might accrue to him professionally or personally for daring to take the unpopular position in the first place.

I witnessed a good example of this fearlessness in 1991. I served as Stanley's host when he visited my institution to stage the first in a series of debates with Dinesh D'Souza about "political correctness" and affirmative action. After the debate, D'Souza sat at a table in the lobby autographing copies of his latest book, and Stanley stood before a line of admirers, answering questions and debating points. As the crowd thinned, I noticed a disheveled, rather sinister-looking man lurking in a corner. When Stanley completed his conversations, he strode over to wait with me; we were to have a cocktail with D'Souza. The mysterious character stepped out of the shadows and walked straight up to Stanley. "It's you Jews who are responsible for the shape this country's in," he exclaimed threateningly. "You own the media and . . ." Fearing that this person represented a clear danger to Stanley, I stepped between them and informed the stranger that we had no time to converse, as we were leaving for an appointment. Always prepared to debate anyone, Stanley gently pushed me aside and exclaimed, "You're right! But you're forgetting something. . . ." And he proceeded to engage this character in a lively discussion. I have no idea if the stranger really did represent a threat, or if Stanley was even aware that this person seemed more interested in confrontation than intellectual conversation; the salient fact is that he has never turned down a good (verbal) fight; it seems to be what he lives for. As he has said more than once, "There are a lot of people out there making mistakes, and I'm just going to tell them that they're making mistakes."

Ironically, this very habit of taking strong stances on unpopular positions, his fearlessness, seems on the surface to work counter to his own psychological need for creating order among chaos; however, it is really just another manifestation of that same need, in that he still understands himself to be setting yet another record straight. Despite the unpopularity of the stance or the consequences flowing from taking it, he is compelled to clear up all misunderstanding, regardless of the consequences.

This compulsion to impose order is intimately linked to a thirst for publicity. He always sought publicity, even as a child. One year when he was still in elementary school, the *Providence Journal* ran a front-page story on the first day of school featuring someone who was just entering the first grade. They chose his sister Rita. The headline, "Rita Goes to School," and the story itself made a deep impression on the fourth grader: he wanted to be publicly celebrated as well. He wanted to be profiled in newspapers and talked about by strangers. He would seek publicity ever since. Even negative publicity was better than none at all; in fact, sometimes negative publicity was the best kind because it furthered his bad-boy reputation and fueled the fascination so many people—in and out of academe—had with the enfant terrible.

While some observers saw his constant search for publicity as egoistic self-promotion, others saw it as a savvy way to further the intellectual causes he cherished while simultaneously advancing his career. Early in his career he developed a habit of sending copies of his articles and books to other scholars around the world. Most academics are notoriously miserly and would never think of spending money to purchase their own books and to mail them to colleagues, but Stanley realized early on that the key to a successful career in the academic world was maximum exposure. A colleague would receive an envelope or package out of the blue containing a neatly typed letter from Stanley saying that he thought the recipient might be interested in his most recent publication. Often this gesture led to letter exchanges over the substance of whatever argument he was making in the publication. This practice of gifting copies of his publications helped him solidify his national reputation early in his career, and he maintained the practice even after he had become internationally famous, but with a different result: recipients of his unexpected gifts were overwhelmed with gratitude that someone of his stature would be so thoughtful and generous as to think of them in this way.

Counterbalancing this fearlessness and constant search for publicity is a surprising vulnerability. Underneath his outward display of self-confidence and even braggadocio is an undercurrent of diffidence. Privately, he very much needs the confirmation of the external world, much more than Jane, who has a strong internal sense of herself. After a public performance of one sort or another, he would often ask those close to him, "How did I do?" He was frequently concerned about what others thought, not of him personally but of his performance. We get a rare glimpse at his internal psychology in a short but revealing statement in the preface to the first edition of *Surprised by Sin*, written in London in 1966. Stanley thanks Adrienne for assisting with the project by typing, editing, and proofreading the manuscript, and he then goes on to state that she had carried the burden of his own daily crises of self-confidence—an odd admission from someone who in public exuded self-confidence almost to a fault—but this unusual moment of vulnerability is perhaps more generally significant and revelatory than it might appear on the surface.

And this private diffidence is not the only trait not in keeping with his public persona. Despite the role of jet-setting academic superstar that he so perfectly inhabited for decades, he hates to travel, and he especially hates to travel alone. He more than once shocked everyone by commenting that "travel narrows," and, in fact, he later wrote a *New York Times* column under that title in which he reveals that he simply is not interested in sightseeing, no matter how exotic the locale, claiming that he was born without the travel gene and perhaps even the curiosity gene. Once when his brother returned from a monthlong trip to South Africa to sightsee and observe the wildlife, he remarked to friends sardonically, "This is something my brother Stanley would *never ever* think of doing. It would be so foreign to him that he would cringe at the idea. He is just not very adventurous in that way." Once when Jane and Stanley visited Ron on St. Kitts, they arranged a tour of the rain forest. Stanley naïvely assumed the trip could be conducted in the comfort of their automobile. To his consternation, it actually involved some walking through thick underbrush. When they returned to his brother's estate after their adventure, he blurted out in his typically loud and effusive manner, a cold cocktail in hand, "I can't believe it! I actually had to climb over a log! A log! I can't believe I had to climb over a log!"

During his time at Hopkins, Stanley and Jane got to be close friends with Kenneth Abraham, the law professor who co-taught a course with Stanley. One summer Jane, Stanley, Abraham, and his wife vacationed together on Kiawah Island, a resort area just outside of Charleston, South Carolina. They rented a bungalow a quarter of a mile from the postcard-perfect beach. Rather than enjoy the white sands and crystal clear ocean, Stanley stayed inside the entire time in front of a little manual typewriter writing the article that he would title "Withholding the Missing Portion: Power, Meaning, and Persuasion in Freud's 'The Wolf-man.'" The others would spend long hours on the beach while he typed furiously on the clunky Royal. Jane came back to the cottage for some sunscreen and said, "Stanley, this is such a gorgeous place. It's so beautiful, why don't you come out to the beach with us?" He looked up from his manuscript and replied, "Jane, that's nature. I don't want to be in nature."

The aura of the urbane superstar that Stanley so meticulously cultivated is not in keeping with his private self—a somewhat diffident, introspective scholar who would gladly trade sunbathing and sightseeing adventures (especially those that entail sweat, heat, and any other bodily discomfort) for the comfort of a quiet, air-conditioned room and a Royal typewriter with a decent ribbon.

Another way that Stanley in his private life was at variance with his persona as the enfant terrible was in his management of money. One might assume given his reputation as a jet-setter who collects expensive luxury cars that he is a freewheeling spendthrift, but this too would be an unfounded assumption. He is both penurious and generous. When it comes to himself, he is parsimonious—buying inexpensive clothes, for example, and penny-pinching on everyday items—but like his father before him he is very generous when someone needs his help. When his aunt and uncle who once lived below them in his boyhood home on Lancaster Street fell ill in their later years, he helped take care of them financially because their own children were not in good enough financial shape to do it alone. He has come to the rescue of other relatives as well. Yet, he would consistently avoid spending money unnecessarily. In 2010 his brother Ron invited Jane and Stanley to visit him on St. Kitts. They were eager to visit Ron on his island paradise until Stanley discovered that the airline tickets would cost $1,100 apiece. While he would easily spend a few grand to help a friend or relative in need, he balked at spending it on a pleasure trip. When Jane contacted Ron to explain that they would have to visit some other time, Ron replied sharply, "Jane, will you please tell my brother that he is not going to live forever and he should spend a little of his millions on himself for a change." In the end, Ron did shame his brother into visiting.

When Walter Benn Michaels first arrived in Chicago to join the faculty at the University of Illinois at Chicago, Stanley volunteered to accompany Michaels and his wife in their apartment-hunting forays. All his life, Stanley loved shopping for real estate deals, and he considered himself quite an authority. Michaels finally settled on a comfortable apartment, but there was just one problem: due to a number of personal circumstances he did not have the money for the hefty down payment. Emulating his father before him, Stanley, without hesitating, pulled out his checkbook and wrote a draft for a substantial amount of money. "I know you're good for this," he said to his friend with a smile. He, of course, expected to be paid back, but he never charged interest.

Generosity aside, Stanley was notorious for being money hungry, reputedly charging more for public speeches than any other humanities professor in the nation, and being able for many years to brag that he was the highest paid English professor in the world (eventually to be overtaken by Henry Louis Gates). While he was interested in making a lot of money, he was almost as interested in assuring that everyone *knew* that he made a lot of money. Money was a visible mark of success for him, and he would often brag about his salary or how much he received for this talk or another. When he was on the Hopkins faculty, he once gave a lecture at another university, and an audience member stood up and asked brusquely why the audience should believe what he was saying. Stanley shot back, "Because I am Stanley Fish, I teach at Johns Hopkins University, and I make seventy-five thousand dollars a year. That's why." To him, the large salary for that time (regardless of whether he actually did make that much) was a visible sign to him of his success and influence, not to mention a weapon to use to bludgeon someone who is out of line.

Often his preoccupation with money had to do more with maintaining his image as the enfant terrible than anything else. When Stanley and Walter Benn Michaels were together at Hopkins and Michaels first arranged to co-teach a course on legal interpretation with their basketball colleague and University of Maryland law professor Ken Abraham, Michaels was to receive compensation of $2,200; this extra compensation was a much-needed windfall. When Michaels told Stanley of his arrangement, Stanley immediately said, "Walter, I would love to be part of that deal. Any way I could co-teach as well?" Michaels was delighted to have his friend be part of the deal but was reluctant to split the money: "Stan, I could really use the twenty-two hundred dollars." To his surprise, Stanley replied, "I don't care about the money." Then he paused for a minute and blurted out, "But you'd better swear never to tell anyone I just said that!" Michaels did promise not to let the secret out that the seemingly money-obsessed literary critic would actually teach a course just for the experience, but then he gleefully reneged, relating the story many times throughout the years.

Stanley may have been unusually skillful for a humanities professor in finding ways to make money, but he was especially adept at managing his money. Late one evening in 2001, months before the tragic events of September 11, he called his good friend Walter Benn Michaels at his home in Baltimore. Michaels used to write about money and financial matters, and Stanley was calling for advice. "Walter, I'm thinking about taking all of my money out of the stock market for a while. I have a very uneasy feeling about the markets for some reason. What do you think?" Although writing about financial issues was a hobby of his friend's, Stanley was not an especially savvy investor himself, certainly no more than the average dabbler in the stock market. "I don't know what to tell you, Stanley," he replied. "You have a much better track record than I do." Stanley followed his instincts and moved hundreds of thousands of dollars out of the market to safety just before the global stock market crashed following the attacks on the Pentagon and the World Trade Center. He saved his fortune. So, Stanley both lived up to his reputation by aggressively accumulating money and countered that reputation by generously giving or loaning it to friends and family in need.

This generosity with money is only one facet of his kindness toward friends and family. Those who know him intimately say he is the "ultimate mensch." When the mother of one of his former graduate students from Hopkins was put in the same retirement home where Jane's mother lived, Stanley would regularly stop in to visit her as well and would spend time talking about her son and his career as a professor. When he would run into the former student at the Modern Language Association convention, he would report on how his mother was doing. His student found it extraordinary that this jet-setting academic superstar would take the time and effort to visit his mother.

Outside of the cutthroat arena of the academy, Stanley is typically very kind. In 1969 when the scholar and novelist David Lodge and his family were to move to Berkeley, where Lodge would serve as a visiting professor, an appointment Stanley had helped engineer, Stanley and Adrienne found the Lodges a house to rent. The house was not immediately available when the Lodges arrived in America, so Stanley and Adrienne, who were out of town at the time, lent the Lodges their own house and one of their cars for a week or so. On Lodge's first day in the Berkeley English department, Stanley was there to introduce him to several colleagues, including the late novelist and short story writer Leonard Michaels, who was teaching at Berkeley at the time. This began another memorable friendship for Lodge, who formally dedicated *Changing Places* to Stanley and Michaels and their wives of that time.

Similarly, when Walter Benn Michaels accepted a position at Johns Hopkins, he purchased a small one-story, two-bedroom house in Mount Washington. The couple were scheduled to move into the new digs in a few days, and Stanley and Adrienne visited to welcome them and tour the house. They all commented on the beautiful hardwood floors, and Stanley asked whether they planned to have them waxed and polished. Michaels was only twenty-seven years old, and this was his first house; it hadn't occurred to him to do anything with the floors. After all, they didn't show signs of wear. "No, we hadn't planned to do anything with the floors," he replied. Stanley smirked and said, "If I loan you the equipment, would you do it?" This sounded like too much work to Michaels, so he declined. "Okay," Stanley answered, emphatically pronouncing each word, "May I come over and do the floors?" So the day before the couple moved in, Stanley arrived with his equipment and spent the whole day waxing and polishing the floors until they were perfect, thereby illustrating not only his typical generosity but his obsession with order and cleanliness.

Stanley may have been a loyal friend to colleagues, but he is especially devoted to his family. Even in his later years after having been married to

Jane for decades, he would frequently reach out and hold her hand when they were out to dinner with friends. And his devotion to his daughter, Susan, is profound and persevering. Susan is naturally introverted and sensitive and has extraordinary social skills. While she has significant artistic talent, she is also skilled at mathematics. She earned a master's degree in math and statistics from North Carolina State and works as a biostatistician for a pharmaceutical company. A serious and committed cyclist, she frequently rides for charity, having three times completed the Life Cycle, a grueling weeklong trek from San Francisco to Los Angeles to raise money for the fight against HIV/AIDS. The ride is so arduous that many have dubbed it the "death cycle." Stanley has always been the doting parent, even long after Susan had grown and had a life of her own.

As a teacher, Stanley is legendary. As soon as he joined the Berkeley faculty, he developed a reputation as a gifted teacher who was energetic, articulate, and exceedingly demanding. He was lively and forceful in his speech and manner, which was novel among the typically sedate professors of the time. His graduate students at Hopkins reported that they went to each class session prepared for battle because he was argumentative and loved participation and challenge; he did not want students to simply agree with him. His class sessions went long, and no one was allowed to leave before class was dismissed. Each session was a command performance. His classes at Hopkins were especially intense because the program was so small and selective. It was not unusual for fifteen students to start the program for the doctorate and for only five to graduate. The competition was fierce, especially for a coveted letter of recommendation from Stanley. The students all jockeyed to demonstrate to him that they were worthy of that letter, further contributing to the intensity.

Throughout the years, he had no tolerance for sloppiness in his students' work. Whether he was teaching first-year composition—which, as dean, he did regularly—or a graduate course, he would simply refuse to accept papers that were not sufficiently well written, grammatically correct, and rhetorically effective. He would begin reading a paper, and if it became clear that the paper exhibited too many problems, he would stop reading it and insist that the student rewrite it. As one colleague commented, "He was completely obsessed with trying to make students write better, and so this was the beginning of his writing on composition issues and how to teach writing."

He expected full attention and participation, as well. An oft-repeated story from his Hopkins days perfectly captures Stanley as the teacher/performer par excellence. He and his good friend and colleague Michael Fried co-taught an undergraduate course on the theory of interpretation, and they were about to begin one session of the class when Fried whispered nervously to his colleague, "Stanley, nearly half the students are not here today." Stanley peered imperiously at the class for a moment and then, as if issuing an edict, announced that attendance was unacceptably low and so he and Professor Fried were going to retire to the cafeteria for a cup of coffee. He sternly instructed the class to go and hunt down every absent student and make sure that the entire class was in attendance for the second hour of the class, which would reconvene promptly at the top of the hour. He made it clear that it was the responsibility of the students to locate their peers and ensure their attendance.

Stanley and Fried sat quietly at a corner table in the cafeteria for a few minutes. Fried seemed a bit shell-shocked; he had never before walked out on a class in this fashion. Stanley took a sip of his coffee and eyed his colleague over the rim of his cup. "What's the matter?" he asked impatiently. "Stanley, what if when we return the students are not there?" Stanley looked intently at him for a moment and replied, "I have no idea. We'll soon find out." Needless to say, the professors returned to a full class. As they entered the room, Stanley winked mischievously at his good friend Fried, who sighed in relief.

Stanley was so genuinely committed to intellectual rigor in the classroom that he applied the same standards to himself. He once shared with Walter Benn Michaels a draft of an article he had written on Holocaust denial. Michaels disagreed with the paper's treatment, and the two engaged in a spirited debate about the topic. The next day Stanley arrived in his undergraduate class at the University of Illinois at Chicago with a stack of copies of his manuscript, which he distributed to the students and announced a writing assignment due the following week: find all the flaws in his essay. This seemed an unprecedented opportunity for these students—to learn where their world-renowned professor might have gone wrong and to be empowered to point it out to him. This was an example of his intellectual commitment as well as his refusal to compromise in his teaching, to dumb down a class or assignment.

Despite his rigor, Stanley treated his students humanely. Over the years he regularly invited his graduate students to social events at his house. He treated his graduate students as colleagues, and they had the opportunity to socialize with faculty and friends as equals. This treatment singled him out in their eyes as special since many professors remained aloof and distant.

While Stanley understands himself to be a superior teacher, he insists—at least in public—that he is not an intellectual. He and Jane have had an ongoing discussion throughout the years about the nature of the intellectual. He has always argued that he himself is not an intellectual. He has consistently felt an outsider in the world of academics, almost a charlatan. The best he could do, he told himself early on in his career, was to do his best to prevail in this erudite world, but he still never quite felt, even in his later years, that academe was his world. This was more naturally the world of his friend Michael O'Loughlin, someone for whom reading himself to sleep with Virgil in the original or some Portuguese epic or Greek romance would be a great pleasure. As Stanley said to Jane many times, "That would *never* occur to me in a million years." Jane, on the other hand, has a much more capacious understanding of the intellectual. For her, an intellectual is someone who is always looking at situations or objects with a certain analytical probing attention, which, Jane would say to her husband, would easily qualify him for the label "intellectual." Despite her line of reasoning, Stanley tenaciously maintains his position. He has even said in print numerous times that his life as a professor is a job: teaching and writing about literature or philosophy or academic institutions is a job—nothing more, nothing less.

Academic work is not something to which he felt a level of dedication that makes it into a religion or a holy cause, as it does for some people. From the beginning he felt that the academic world was not his world by inheritance or cultural education, but, nevertheless, it was the world he found himself in and so was going to have to make his way by figuring out how to do that work well.

This attitude is reflected in his view, for example, of academic freedom, where, for him, academic freedom is a guild notion; that is, it is the academic's version of a desire that all professionals and even some nonprofessional workers have to be in a position to dictate their own working conditions and be free of monitoring or assessment by others.

He has always felt that professors are hired to do a job, are assigned a particular task, work in one of the institutional spaces in which this task is performed, and are paid to perform this task. He is comfortable arguing for academic freedom in *those* terms, as desirable conditions of the workplace, but he refuses to argue for it, as so many people do, as some kind of extension, first, of the First Amendment concept of freedom of expression and, also, of the Platonic, Socratic search for Truth, a project in which professors are invested with a kind of privileged status that cannot be claimed by other professions. "I've never been able to even hear that argument with a straight face," he once told a colleague. "It just doesn't make any sense."

Perhaps his feeling that he is not a true intellectual is embedded in his blue-collar upbringing, where working is a matter of survival, not an avocation as it might be for someone from a more affluent background—and the profession of English professor in his day was full of such individuals.

As an intellectual and a writer, Stanley was especially influenced by the work of Augustine, J. L. Austin, and C. S. Lewis. He admired the way Lewis wrote, particularly his lucid prose style. He thought it was a style that was at once powerful and accessible. It had a strong moral urgency that he admired. While he did emulate the clear prose of Lewis and Augustine, he was not intellectually adventurous, in the way that some of his contemporaries were; he has not attempted to articulate some grand, panoramic way of seeing the world. In contrast to major theorists such as Northrop Frye, Harold Bloom, Michel Foucault, and Jacques Derrida—figures who might be mentioned in the same breath as Fish—or theorists whose work was suffused with a combination of aesthetic and ideological energy, such as Edward Said, Terry Eagleton, Jacques Lacan, Louis Althusser, or Gilles Deleuze and Felix Guattari, Stanley consistently focused narrowly on specific issues in the theory of interpretation or in interpreting a specific literary work.

His philosophy of scholarly work—or at least what has worked for him—is that if you begin with a topic or problem that is intellectually interesting to you and you maintain a narrow focus, you might in the end arrive at something larger and more ambitious 'in conception; but if you start off with something more ambitious in conception, you run the risk of becoming overwhelmed by your project. "I always think of myself as being much more narrow in scope than my contemporaries in the literary-cultural-critical world are," he told a colleague. "I'm less ambitious to develop a grand scheme of some kind or to draw sweeping panoramas."

Given this narrowness of scope, he always felt that, as a scholar, he was more like his friends Gerald Graff, E. D. Hirsch, and Barbara Herrnstein Smith than like Harold Bloom or the Continental postmodern theorists. He approaches scholarly work in the same way he does his *New York Times* column: "Let's look closely at how this particular argument works."

The essence of how he approaches intellectual work is that he loves to explain things. This compulsion to explain the world is precisely what attracts him to teaching and to writing. He loves to begin with some well-defined problem and to unpack it and explain it. So, his advice to novice scholars is always to overexplain the subject at hand, whereas he feels that many of his contemporaries underexplain things or are cryptic. No one who has read Stanley's work carefully has ever accused him of being cryptic.

One work habit that has paid dividends for Stanley over the years is that whenever he attends a lecture or talk, he takes extensive notes, complete with dotted lines connecting points, numbers indicating how to get from one argument to another, and rejoinders when appropriate. This practice has helped him consistently ask the most incisive questions and advance the most cogent responses in the question-and-answer sessions that typically follow such talks. Once in the late 1970s he happened to be in New York City and learned that the eminent scholar Meyer Abrams was scheduled to give a talk at Columbia University on poststructuralist theory, so he went to hear the talk. It turned out to be a focused attack on the work of Jacques Derrida, Harold Bloom, and Stanley. As usual, Stanley took copious notes. When the question-and-answer session began, someone in the audience stood up and announced, "Dr. Abrams, a member of your infernal trio is in fact here in the audience." Abrams then made the tactical error of inviting Stanley up to the podium to give a response. With the help of his elaborate notes, Stanley launched into a full-scale explication and refutation of Abrams's entire talk, point by point. It was a tour de force. Stanley's rebuttal was so thorough and successful that, during all the years he knew Abrams afterwards, he could not convince him that he had not seen his paper in advance. Abrams simply refused to believe that anyone could be that thorough and coherent in an impromptu response.

While he never avoided a controversy about academic subjects, Stanley has always assiduously avoided politics in his written works and in his public discussions. He was once given the opportunity to weigh in on the Israeli-Palestinian problem; he declined. People on the political right have regularly called him a left-wing radical; people on the left a conservative apologist. The *New York Times* once reported that he was a registered Republican; however, he generously donated more than once to the Clinton-Gore campaign. In his early days at Berkeley some colleagues speculated that he supported Barry Goldwater for president in 1964; after all, he hated 1960s activism and refused to cancel his classes so that students could participate in campus free-speech protests. Yet, while at Duke he was the darling of those who supported political correctness, and he vigorously fought that fight. (His brother Ron would tease him by purposely making sexist comments, hoping to get a rise out of his older brother. Stanley never took the bait.) Later in his career he infuriated progressive academics by arguing—first in *Professional Correctness* and then in *Save the World on Your Own Time*—that a course in English studies is no place to attempt to address political agendas. He once commented that liberals are silly and foolish while conservatives are a bunch of thugs. Nobody has yet successfully cubbyholed him into a neat political ideology.

In a certain way, politics is not important to him, or at least is not high on his priority list. When he was an administrator and was hiring people, he never cared about the candidates' political backgrounds, whether they were conservative or liberal; he only really cared about whether they were smart. His bottom line has always been the same: is the person demonstrably intelligent. This refusal to factor in people's political allegiances is why he could be good friends both with arch-conservative Dinesh D'Souza and with Marxist critic Fredric Jameson.

While Stanley enjoys a comfortable life teaching at Florida International University and the Cardozo School of Law, giving invited lectures across the nation and abroad, writing his *New York Times* column, and splitting his time among his three homes, some close friends and former colleagues speculate that in his later years Stanley has been somewhat depressed or melancholic. At the very least, a spark that was uniquely his seems to be missing. Friends report that when they meet him for dinner, he seems vaguely absent, uninterested in the conversation, or participating just enough not to seem rude. Some detect an aura of sadness about him. If this is in fact a fair assessment, there are several likely explanations. The height of his career corresponded with the heyday of high theory. It is hard to overstate the intellectual excitement of the times—the years between the mid-1960s and the mid-1990s. Those who participated felt that they were in or at least witnessing a movement—something akin to a social movement like the women's or civil rights movements, only in the academic world. In fact, the academic movement directly supported and furthered the progressive social movements of the time. Stanley, of course, was a central figure in that intellectual movement. Although scholars continue to produce interesting and at times exciting theoretical work to this day, absent is the sense that everyone is participating in an intellectual revolution, a radical rejection of commonly held beliefs and ways of understanding the world. During the three decades or so of high theory's ascendancy, Stanley was ever present—a must-read essayist, a much-sought-after speaker and lecturer, and a guru and role model for a generation of aspiring intellectuals. While the academic world has always had some version of celebrity scholars, this has always been on a muted, understated scale. In the theory days, in contrast, the academic superstars were larger than life, almost small-scale versions of Hollywood film stars. This is precisely why David Lodge's novels about academic life were so popular and why a movie version of his *Changing Places* was in development for several years. (The producer tried in vain to cast Walter Matthau in the role of Morris Zapp, and Stanley let it be known that he would love the opportunity to play the role himself.) Never before in modern times have scholars enjoyed the kind of public spotlight that they did in those heady years.

This book began with a description of a scene in 1991 when a standing-room-only crowd packed a huge university auditorium to watch a debate between Stanley and conservative author Dinesh D'Souza. It is no exaggeration to say that the event had the feel and flavor of a major sporting event, like a prizefight in boxing. In fact, the event organizers were even using the vocabulary of boxing at the time—directing the two debaters not to pull any punches and to go for a knockout blow. There was an electricity in the air not typical of a traditional academic debate. It certainly had a similar kind of drama: two heavyweight stars, anticipation and perhaps even anxiety over who might "win," and riotous applause when one or the other landed a well-placed zinger.

This was Stanley's world at its height. He was frequently the center of attention—something he always craved and relished. Like a real prize-fighter, he was admired by many and despised by others. Obviously, it is difficult to sustain this high level of celebrity over a long period of time. The interest in high theory waned; its newness—and therefore its revolutionary nature—faded with time; and many of the theory superstars passed away or passed into obscurity. By the end of 2004 most of the central figures associated with theory had died: Althusser, Barthes, Bourdieu, Deleuze, Derrida, Guattari, Foucault, Lacan, Lyotard, and Said. In 2007, both Baudrillard and Rorty would pass away as well. Theory's heyday, like that of its main proponents, was over. Stanley survived all of these theorists, but like a retired prizefighter—someone who can no longer get in the ring but must stand on the sidelines as a spectator—he no longer enjoyed the limelight that he once did. For someone who craves the kind of attention that he has throughout his long career, this is certainly a sad state of affairs.

And, undoubtedly, another cause of disappointment for Stanley is that he was never able to secure an appointment as a university president—once an active goal of his. In commenting on the aura of melancholy that seems to have descended on Stanley, an old friend stated, "I think he would love to be running a major institution and living in a beautiful apartment overlooking Central Park or George Washington Park bought by the institution for him, but he does not have those things." Since the final days of his deanship at the University of Illinois at Chicago, he interviewed for countless presidencies and was a finalist in several presidential searches, but the fit never seemed right for him. It is likely that this unrealized ambition contributes to any existential sadness that may be affecting him.

These disappointments aside, by anyone else's standards, Stanley's later career has been quite successful—he has had a coveted position as a *New York Times* columnist and a named professorship at a respectable university within easy driving distance from one of his homes; he published a popular book on the television series *The Fugitive*, a best-selling book on crafting sentences, a book on the poetry of Milton and others, and a book on academic freedom. He still maintains a rigorous schedule of public speeches and lectures. Perhaps, most important, he has built a rich and enduring legacy: he is already in the history books as one of the twentieth century's most original and influential intellectuals. Surely Max would crack a rare smile and say, "Not bad, son. Not bad."

Chronology

1938	Born April 19 in Providence, Rhode Island.
1951	Bar mitzvahed May 5.
1955	Graduated from Classical High School.
1955–59	Attended University of Pennsylvania as an undergraduate.
1959	Graduated from University of Pennsylvania with a BA.
1959	Married Adrienne Aaron August 23.
1959–62	Attended graduate school at Yale University.
1960	Awarded MA in English from Yale.
1962	Awarded PhD in English from Yale.
1962	Appointed instructor at University of California at Berkeley.
1963	Appointed assistant professor at Berkeley.
1963	Taught Milton for first time when Berkeley's Miltonist, C. A. Patrides, was awarded a grant.
1965	Yale University Press published *John Skelton's Poetry*.
1966	Awarded American Council of Learned Societies Fellowship.
1967	Promoted to associate professor.
1967	Harvard University published *Surprised by Sin: The Reader in "Paradise Lost."*
1967	Appointed visiting assistant professor at Washington University.
1969	Promoted to professor.
1969	Spent summer in Paris studying poststructuralist theory.
1969	Awarded Guggenheim Fellowship.
1969	Appointed visiting professor at Sir George Williams University.

173

1971	Appointed visiting professor at Johns Hopkins University.
1971	Oxford University Press published *Seventeenth Century Prose: Modern Essays in Criticism*.
1971	Appointed visiting professor in the Linguistics Institute at SUNY Buffalo.
1972	University of California Press published *Self-Consuming Artifacts: The Experience of Seventeenth Century Literature*.
1972	*Self-Consuming Artifacts* nominated for National Book Award.
1973–74	Appointed visiting Leo S. Bing Professor of English at University of Southern California.
1974	Directed National Endowment for the Humanities Summer Seminar on Critical Theory.
1974–85	Appointed professor of English at Johns Hopkins University.
1976	Directed National Endowment for the Humanities Summer Seminar on Critical Theory.
1976–85	Appointed adjunct professor of law at University of Maryland Law School.
1977	Taught graduate course in recent trends in literary theory at Temple University, where he met Jane Tompkins.
1977	Taught at School of Criticism and Theory Summer Institute at University of California at Irvine.
1978	The University of California Press published *The Living Temple: George Herbert and Catechizing*.
1978–85	Appointed William Kenan Jr. Professor of English and Humanities at Johns Hopkins University.
1980	Divorced Adrienne (Aaron) Fish.
1980	Harvard University Press published *Is There a Text in This Class? Interpretive Communities and the Sources of Authority*.
1980	Directed National Endowment for the Humanities Summer Seminar on Milton and Critical Theory.
1982	Married Jane Tompkins on August 7.
1982	Directed National Endowment for the Humanities Summer Seminar on Milton and Critical Theory.

1983–84	Appointed visiting professor at Columbia University.
1983–85	Served as department chair at Johns Hopkins University.
1985	Inducted into American Academy of Arts and Sciences.
1985–98	Appointed Arts and Sciences Professor of English and Law at Duke University.
1986–92	Served as chair of the Department of English at Duke.
1989	Duke University Press published *Doing What Comes Naturally: Change, Rhetoric, and the Practice of Theory in Literary and Legal Studies.*
1989	Appointed fellow of Humanities Institute at the University of California at Irvine.
1989	Received Milton Society of America's James Holly Hanford Award for the best essay published in 1989.
1991	Began national debate tour with Dinesh D'Souza.
1991	Named Honored Scholar by Milton Society of America.
1993–98	Appointed executive director of Duke University Press.
1993–98	Appointed associate vice provost at Duke University.
1994	Oxford University Press published *There's No Such Thing as Free Speech, and It's a Good Thing, Too.*
1994	Received the PEN/Spielvogel-Diamonstein Award for *There's No Such Thing as Free Speech, and It's a Good Thing, Too.*
1995	Oxford University Press published *Professional Correctness: Literary Studies and Political Change.*
1995	Appointed distinguished visiting faculty fellow at Center for Ideas and Society at the University of California at Riverside.
1995	Appointed adjunct professor of law at Columbia University.
1997	Harvard University Press published the thirtieth anniversary edition of *Surprised by Sin: The Reader in "Paradise Lost."*
1997	Thirtieth anniversary edition of *Surprised by Sin* wins the Milton Society of America's James Holly Hanford Book Award.
1999	Blackwell published *The Stanley Fish Reader*, edited by H. Aram Veeser.

1999	Harvard University Press published *The Trouble with Principle.*
1999–2004	Served as dean of the College of Liberal Arts and Sciences at University of Illinois at Chicago.
2000–2	Served as distinguished visiting professor at the John Marshall Law School.
2001	Harvard University Press published *How Milton Works.*
2001–5	Served as monthly columnist for the *Chronicle of Higher Education.*
2004–5	Named Dean Emeritus and UIC Distinguished Professor at University of Illinois at Chicago.
2005	Appointed Davidson-Kahn Distinguished University Professor of Humanities and Law at Florida International University.
2008	Oxford University Press published *Save the World on Your Own Time.*
2010	Appointed to Board of Visitors of Ralston College.
2011	The University of Pennsylvania Press published *The Fugitive in Flight: Faith, Liberalism, and Law in a Classic TV Show.*
2011	HarperCollins published *How to Write a Sentence: And How to Read One.*
2012	Cambridge University Press published *Versions of Antihumanism: Milton and Others.*
2013	Appointed Floersheimer Distinguished Visiting Professor at the Benjamin N. Cardozo School of Law.
2014	The University of Chicago Press published *Versions of Academic Freedom: From Professionalism to Revolution* (The Rice University Campbell Lectures).
2014	Cambridge University Press published *Stanley Fish on Philosophy, Politics and Law: How Fish Works* by Michael Robertson.
2015	Princeton University Press published *Think Again: Contrarian Reflections on Life, Politics, Religion, Law, and Education.*